kisses *of* sunshine

for women

Other Books in the Kisses of Sunshine Series

Kisses of Sunshine for Grandmas
by Carol Kent and Gracie Malone
Kisses of Sunshine for Moms
by Carol Kent and Ellie Kay
Kisses of Sunshine for Sisters
by Carol Kent
Kisses of Sunshine for Teachers
by Carol Kent and Vicki Caruana

carol kent . thelma wells

kisses *of* sunshine
for women

GRAND RAPIDS, MICHIGAN 49530 USA

ZONDERVAN™

Kisses of Sunshine for Women
Copyright © 2005 by Speak Up, Inc., and Thelma Wells

Requests for information should be addressed to:
Zondervan, *Grand Rapids, Michigan 49530*

Library of Congress Cataloging-in-Publication Data

Kisses of sunshine for women / [compiled by] Carol Kent and Thelma Wells.
  —1st ed.
        p. cm.
    Summary: "This devotional provides sources of hope for readers"—
Provided by the publisher.
  ISBN-10: 0-310-24768-3 (hardcover)
  ISBN-13: 978-0-310-24768-5
  1. Christian women—Prayer-books and devotions—English. I. Kent,
  Carol, 1947– II. Wells, Thelma, 1941–
  BV4844.K572 2005
  242'.643—dc22   2004028854

This edition printed on acid-free paper.

The website addresses recommended are offered as a resource to you. These websites are not intended in any way to be or imply an endorsement on the part of Zondervan, nor do we vouch for their content for the life of this book.

Published in association with the literary agency of Alive Communications, Inc., 7680 Goddard Street, Suite 200, Colorado Springs, CO 80920.

Interior design by Tracey Walker

Printed in the United States of America

05 06 07 08 09 10 11 12 /❖ DCI/ 10 9 8 7 6 5 4 3 2 1

To my granddaughters and my great-granddaughter:
Vanessa C. Wells
Alaya L. Cohen
Alyssa E. Wells
Bryna A. Cohen
Auriana M. Cox

THELMA WELLS

. . . .

To women who make a positive difference in my life:
Anne Denmark
Cathy Gallagher
Janet Fleck
Ginger Shaw
Kathe Wunnenberg

CAROL KENT

contents

introduction

This *Kisses of Sunshine* series of five books — one each for women, moms, sisters, grandmas, and teachers — has lighthearted, uplifting, often humorous stories meant to bring a sunburst of joy to your life — as you remember that God loves you. Thelma Wells, beloved Women of Faith speaker and author, has joined me in putting the stories in this book together, and our purpose is simply to let God's love so warm and fill you that you become warmth, light, and love to the people around you.

There's nothing quite as comforting as reading the stories of women who allow us to laugh out loud at their crazy antics, empathize with their imperfect choices, feel their hurts, celebrate their successes, and point us to the truth of God's Word. This book is for women of all ages who are interested in personal and spiritual growth.

Thelma's stories teach us how to embrace our worth to ourselves and to God. She brings us to an understanding of his role in erasing the baggage of shame and guilt we may be dragging around. She says, "It's wonderful to know we don't have to live with silent, private guilt all of our lives. What may have happened in your past is over and should be done with. It's history. You can pack your guilt and shame away in a box, use duct tape around the edges to seal it tightly, and put it in the trash where it belongs . . . because Jesus wants you to bring it to him."

Some of these stories will make you laugh out loud and others will make you dry a tear. Thelma and I pray this book will nurture your soul as it leads you to fresh faith, renewed hope, and purposeful living. We are grateful to the publishing team at Zondervan for giving us the opportunity of working on such an enjoyable project, and we are especially thankful to our executive editor, Sandra Vander Zicht, for her visionary leadership and compassionate coaching during the writing process.

I also want to thank the remarkable women who shared their stories in this book. You inspired, motivated, and encouraged me — but most of all, you reminded me that my goal in life is not perfection. Your genuine authenticity will help every reader to be "the real deal" in her relationships with others. Happy reading!

— CAROL KENT, GENERAL EDITOR

he knows my name

Thelma Wells

- -

The beginning of wisdom is to call things by their right names.

CHINESE PROVERB

y mother was little more than a child herself when, at age seventeen, she gave birth to me. Not only was she young, she was crippled and unmarried. In scribbled handwriting, from the back room of my grandparents' home in Dallas, Texas, she wrote "Baby Girl Morris" on my birth certificate. However, she called me "Thelma" after the midwife who helped deliver me. Later I assumed the distinctive last name of "Smith" from my biological father.

It wasn't until I applied for a passport to take a trip to Panama that I encountered a real problem, when all I could produce was a birth certificate that read "Baby Girl Morris." I had to spend $175 in a court of law to buy the name I had used all my life.

Not many women can say, "I was a girl without a name," but I meet ladies every day who have no idea who they really are. It is one of the greatest privileges of my life to be able to say (and write a book with the title), *Girl, Have I Got Good News for You!*

One aspect of sharing God's love with women that I most enjoy is helping them regain their self-esteem. I get so excited as I am able to "midwife" them into an understanding of God's role in erasing the baggage of shame and guilt they may be dragging around. I tell them, "You don't have to live with silent, private guilt all of your life. What may have happened in your past is over and should be done with. It's history. You can pack your guilt and shame away in a box, use duct tape around the edges to seal it tightly, and put it in the trash where it belongs, because Jesus wants you to bring it to him."

And after I have delivered this good news, I tell them they have a new name. They are not a nobody, they are not a generic Baby Girl Doe in their Father's eyes. He calls them by a holy name. They are blessed, redeemed, and precious. They are his lambs, daughters of the king, his bride.

I paid $175 for a piece of paper that says my name is Thelma Wells.

Jesus paid with his life, on a cross, to give me a new name written in the Book of Life. Today I happily and legally go by the earth name of "Thelma," but I know my true identity, my heavenly name is "Daughter of God, Beloved and Forgiven."

....

Fear not, for I have redeemed you;
I have summoned you by name; you are mine.

ISAIAH 43:1

a surprise in the closet

Shari Minke

All that we send into the lives of others comes back into our own.

REMINISCE MAGAZINE

*U*gh! I tried pushing the hangers in my bedroom closet. Curling my fingers behind the metal rod I felt the obstacle preventing my success. I pulled out a wad — it was two crumpled ten-dollar bills! Instantly my fingers went into search mode feeling for more "wads." Ha! I discovered another one, then another, and another! Laughter bubbled out of me as I threw money on the floor. I dropped to the floor, flattened the money, and counted.

I rushed to the phone and called my husband. "You'll never guess what just happened! I found $800 in our closet!" Tom was as stunned as I was.

"What do we do with the money?" I asked.

Tom chuckled. "Call your Dad — he's a wise man — but the first thing I want you to do is to check *all* the closets!"

Finding no more money, I called my father. Dad's counsel was this: "According to the law, when you purchase a house, all its contents become your property, so legally, the money is yours. But you have to ask yourself, 'What is the *ethical* thing to do?' Ask God. He will show you what he wants you to do with the money."

Seven years earlier we had purchased our home from a man named Fred. We learned that Fred built the home for his wife. It was their "dream house." After they lived in the home for only two years, Fred's wife died of cancer. He left the house empty for another two years, unable to bear the thought of selling it.

During the seven years we lived in the house, Fred had passed away. Fred's daughter, Judy, lived in our subdivision. I struggled with whether the money should go to Judy.

I told God honestly, "I really want this money. You know it would help with our current cost of finishing the basement, but what do *you* want me to do with it? Please show me."

A few days later while reading my Bible, words on the page seemed to blaze like neon lights, "Keep your lives free from the love of money and *be content with what you have*" (Hebrews 13:5).

In that moment I had the answer. God also impressed on my heart this message:

Wait. I will tell you when to give Judy the money.

The following Sunday I felt like a bolt of lightning hit me. God spoke to my heart saying, *Go! Go now!* I jumped off the couch, stuffed the money in my pocket, and said to Tom, "I'm going to Judy's house!"

When Judy opened the door, I could see she had been crying. I asked if I could come in, and she graciously invited me inside.

"Judy, a couple of weeks ago while I was moving the clothes in my closet, I discovered some money hidden up under the rod."

Dropping her head, she smiled, "That would have been my mother."

I pulled the large wad of bills out of my pocket and said, "Well, this money belongs to you."

Judy sat stunned for a moment as I placed the bundle in her hands. Stammering, as though coming out of shock, Judy shook her head, "Uh, no, wait, you found the money, it belongs to you."

"No, Judy, the money belongs to *you*," I assured her.

Tears streamed down her face. "I've been alone for a while. It's not often that my husband and kids are out at the same time. Just before you came over, I was missing my mother so badly I walked into the family room and took a picture of her off the wall. As I was holding the picture, I said aloud to God, 'Please, just let me know my mom is okay.' Then you showed up at the door."

Now both of us were crying!

For seven years I had shifted the seasonal clothes in my closet. Never had the hidden wads of money hindered me. How inconceivable that God knew a day would come when Judy would be missing her mother so terribly and call out to him for comfort. God was there, waiting to answer her call.

Two weeks later Judy and her husband showed up on our doorstep. Smiling, Judy handed me an envelope and said, "We feel you should have half of the money. You didn't have to tell us about finding it. We want to share the gift!"

Gratefully we received the money and used it to help remodel her parents' "dream house."

So in everything, do to others what you would have them do to you.

MATTHEW 7:12

the lost keys

Jennie Afman Dimkoff

··

Always . . . set a high value on spontaneous kindness.

SAMUEL JOHNSON

*B*ernie, will you go back to the van for more product?" I asked, handing her the keys. "We're already getting low on stock, and the crowd after the parade will be unbelievable."

I owned a small art business for fifteen years, and one of the best aspects of the work included exhibiting our wares at several upscale outdoor arts and crafts shows throughout the summer. One of my favorite events was the Coast Guard Festival held annually in Grand Haven, Michigan. With thousands of people pouring into the beautiful port city, the show was so busy I always had to hire extra staff. For this particular show I had hired Bernadine to tend the booth with me. She was one of my dearest and most fun friends.

"I'll hold things down here while you're gone, but hurry, okay?" I added, feeling a bit overwhelmed at the thought of waiting on a lineup of customers without the aid of an assistant.

Bernie was gone for a *long* time. When she finally returned, my normally vivacious, fun-loving friend seemed very subdued. Setting my keys down beside my briefcase, she quietly went about restocking the tables.

I watched Bernie, perplexed by my friend's unusual demeanor, and noticed a dark blue stain on the edge of her right sleeve, which was rolled up high on her arm.

"Bernie, what in the world did you get on your blouse?"

A stricken look crossed her face and, yanking at the sleeve in question, she burst into tears, words tumbling out on top of each other.

"Oh, Jennie, it was awful! On my way to the van I passed a row of port-a-potties and figured it would be wise to make use of the facilities right then, rather than decide I needed to stop after I was loaded down with product, so I did."

Bewildered by her distress, I nodded, while she, in great agitation, continued with her story.

"Well, just as I was turning to leave the cubicle, I heard something *awful*. It was the sound of your keys hitting the toilet seat! I stood there in shock for a moment, and then I opened the door to tell the people who were waiting that they simply *couldn't* go inside, because I'd dropped my keys down the hole and had to get them back!"

She went on breathlessly, "A man from the line kindly went to his car and came back with a coat hanger, and I fished and I fished!"

My mind was racing as I took in what my friend was saying.

"And finally," she went on anxiously, "in desperation, I held my breath and closed my eyes and I reached down and *got* them! Then I raced to a gas station, and thank goodness there was hot water and soap! I scrubbed my hands and arm until my skin felt raw. And, Jennie, I swear I let scalding water run on your keys for at least ten minutes!"

As I stared at my friend in horror, two things became clear to me. First, her act of sacrifice for me that day was very likely *greater* than what I could have done in return. And second, it was best *not* to tell her that I had a second set of keys in my purse.

Later, after the Coast Guard parade, various politicians who had taken part in the event circulated throughout the large art fair, meeting and greeting potential voters. The governor of Michigan stopped by our booth and warmly greeted each of us. After he left, Bernie turned to me with her first real smile of the afternoon.

"Well," she said with a grin while looking down at her right hand, "I figured it was best *not* to tell the governor where the hand he just shook had been earlier today."

Thinking back on that day, I have marveled over having a friend who would go to such great lengths to help me. How could she have done what she did? Then I am reminded of Jesus Christ, the dearest of friends, who was willing to do the most radical act of friendship for me. He suffered shame, scorn, and pain, and he then laid down his life for me.

. . . .

Greater love has no one than this,
that he lay down his life for his friends.

JOHN 15:13

the blue shepherd

Edna Ellison

· ·

Your flesh prays little prayers. God is able to do more than we ask.

JENNIFER KENNEDY DEAN

One Sunday morning in the '60s, I'd cooked and served breakfast, spilled milk in the refrigerator and wiped it out, and was mopping the dribbles off the floor when Jack, our teenaged son, needed to iron out a wrinkle. To speed up the process, I set up the ironing board, steam-pressed the wrinkle, and creased the pants as quickly as I could. I finally headed out the door, hurrying Jack, his sister Patsy, age thirteen, and their father to the car.

Since that morning's Bible study was long, I taught my Sunday school class at ninety miles per hour, with gusts up to a hundred! Afterward I tried not to seem rushed as a visitor lingered at the door. Then I ran down the hallway, stripping off my jacket, and, in the choir room, jumped into my choir robe, entering the sanctuary with the rest of the choir. Some of them — good friends — mumbled a joke about changing clothes and "streaking." I laughed and then sang with as much air power as I could muster, but I was tired.

After church we finished the biggest meal of the week. Two hours and a chicken carcass later, as I washed dishes, Patsy said, "Mom, Mrs. Franklin called yesterday, and we are having a dress rehearsal for the Christmas pageant this afternoon at five o'clock."

I laid the dishcloth down, greasy from the gravy pan.

"Patsy, the Christmas pageant is two weeks away. We'll be ready on time." I longed for the couch and a few minutes' rest.

"But, Mom, tonight is dress rehearsal. Allison is a beige shepherd, and I'm a blue shepherd."

"Surely Mrs. Franklin is not expecting all of you in costumes two weeks before the performance."

"She came in our Sunday school class again this morning and said it's really easy. We just need a blue piece of cloth with rough edges, no hemming. Just sew, sloping down the shoulders, and leave an opening for a boat neckline and armholes, like a caftan."

Easy for her to say, I thought. I looked toward heaven. *Lord, save me from having to sew a shepherd's costume today*, I prayed.

"C'mon, Patsy," I said a few moments later. "Let's see if we have any fabric." We looked in a closet where we store cloth: pink-flowered piquet, polka-dotted green silk, yellow stripes, but no blue cloth suitable for a shepherd. Then I remembered. Months before, a student had left a bag with blue cloth in my

English classroom at the school where I taught. If we could find it, I might whip it into a costume in a few hours, but I wasn't sure where it was. It had been on a lost-and-found table outside my classroom until the principal asked us to clean up for a PTA meeting. I'd asked a student to put it in a file cabinet, but I had not checked to see where she placed it.

I called the school secretary to get a key to the school, and Patsy and I headed for her house. On the way, she said, "Oh, Mom, I also need a scarf the same color as the shepherd's robe and a blue rope to tie around it to make a head cover."

I laughed. "Blue rope! Have you ever seen a blue rope? Impossible!" She laughed too and shrugged her shoulders.

We entered the school using the secretary's key and walked the dark corridors to my room. As we dug into the lost-and-found junk in the file drawers, there it was — a bag with blue polyester cloth. Imagine our surprise when I shook it out and found a flowing caftan — a perfect shepherd's costume, with a boat neckline, sloping shoulders, and loose armholes. Patsy tried it on, and it fit perfectly!

"Look, Mom," she said. She lifted out a scarf that fit, hanging below her shoulders. Then she pulled out the unbelievable: a blue rope, long enough to tie around her head, making a perfect shepherd's head cover!

I don't know how that costume appeared just when we needed it. Did a home economics student sew it months before and then decide that a caftan wasn't her style? Did God miraculously zap it in the drawer that day? I know only that he answered the prayer of a tired mother who prayed, "Lord, save me from having to make a shepherd's costume today," and he did it his way — far above anything I could have imagined.

. . . .

Now to him who is able to do immeasurably more than all we ask or imagine, according to his power that is at work within us, to him be glory in the church and in Christ Jesus throughout all generations, for ever and ever! Amen.

EPHESIANS 3:20–21

birth of a friendship

Cheryl Gochnauer

. . . .

Shared grief is half the sorrow,
but happiness when shared, is doubled.

AUTHOR UNKNOWN

ismay blanketed the office as news spread from cubicle to cubicle: the wife of one of our favorite coworkers had just lost her baby.

Jack's workstation was silent, a darkened room with shadows falling on family photos and his three-year-old son's crayon masterpieces. As employees whispered, I slipped into the bathroom and wiped empathetic tears for his wife, Suzanne. I had miscarried the year before and understood the grief of preempted parenting.

I also knew the frustration of fielding inane comments from people who mean to help but trample tender hearts instead. "It was God's will." "You'll have more children." "At least you weren't too far along." These and other phrases had left me feeling even more bereft.

Like Suzanne, I had a preschooler at home to hug me, to smile, and to remind me of exactly what I had lost. So though I'd never met Suzanne, I wrote this young Christian mother a letter which said all the things I wished someone had said to me.

Suzanne wrote back. Our friendship was instant and deep, a sisterly bond forged by common hurt and common belief in the One who shared our troubles. Over the following year, we spent lots of time together, a couple of modern-day Hannahs trying to catch God's attention, and eventually the giggles outweighed the tears.

As we were about to discover, our Father was listening to every word.

"I'm going to have a baby!" Suzanne's bubbly voice danced over the phone line. I celebrated like I was the one who was pregnant.

A week later, I was.

"No way!" But there it was. The test strip was bright blue.

While Suzanne dove into preparations for her coming child, I held back. *What if something happens to this baby?*

But Suzanne would have none of that. As I had once prompted her, she pushed me toward the Giver of Life. My hesitation gave way to cautious optimism, then to joyful planning of my own.

One sunny September afternoon, Carrie Marie arrived, healthy and perfect. As I stood over the birthing room bassinet admiring her shining red hair, a familiar face appeared beside me. "Hey, neighbor!" Jack beamed. "We're right next door!"

Within the hour, I was walking the hospital halls with Suzanne and Jack as my newborn slept. In true been-there, done-that fashion, I cheered Suzanne on as she waddled along, clutching her contracting belly. "You're gonna do great!"

And she did. A few hours later, I held Carrie to my breast and listened as Suzanne gave one last push in the adjoining birthing room. Garrett Neal squalled a robust hello as I laughed out loud and thanked God not only for his mercy but also for his impeccable timing.

A dozen years have passed since that glorious day when God filled both our arms with cherub-cheeked treasure. Suzanne and I now smile at our precocious preteens and their equally adored older siblings, keenly aware of how special each one of them is . . .

. . . just like our other children, who are playing at Jesus' house until their mommies come home.

. . . .

For the Lord is good and his love endures forever;
his faithfulness continues through all generations.

PSALM 100:5

queen bee

Thelma Wells

. . . .

Don't even try to bury me without my bumblebee pin!

THELMA WELLS

hen guests walk into the large sunroom in my home, they are often attacked by a swarm of bees. Not live bees, mind you, but plush bees, paper bees, toy bees, and ceramic bees. I have bee coffee mugs, bee paperweights, bee potholders, and my prize—a diamond bee broach. I even have a bumblebee toilet seat!

If there is an item with a bee attached to it, Honey (no pun intended), I've probably bought it, received it as a gift, or created it.

Why this obsession with bees?

Years ago, I happened upon some startling information. I learned that the humble bumblebee is scientifically too big, its wingspan too narrow, for it to fly. Yet it buzzes around anyway doing what God made it to do. Like the bumblebee, I didn't come into the world equipped to fly. As you've already learned, I began life with so many strikes against me that I should be a welfare statistic or hopelessly emotionally scarred.

But the miraculous power of God became the wind beneath this chubby little girl's wings and taught her to fly in spite of all that logic would dictate. I was born into poverty, but with God's grace I graduated from college and became a corporate speaker for the banking industry. I wasn't even given a legal name when I was born, but now I speak to thousands of women, telling them of their truest identity, and of a Father who has loved them from the moment they came into existence.

In the days of segregation I learned what it was like to be hated and mistreated because of the color of my skin. I could have refused to associate with white people as a way to get my revenge. Today, I minister as the only black woman on the Women of Faith team, speaking to audiences of every color and race.

My marriage suffered more than enough blows to have easily and almost predictably ended in divorce, but with God's amazing grace — and two wounded people willing to do the work of restoration — George and I have not only stayed married for forty years but we each still think the other is the cutest thing walking around on two legs. I've survived nearly every heartbreak a mother can anticipate with a prodigal child, but today that prodigal is a productive citizen and loving parent. I do not mean to imply that all is perfect, for no human relationships are ever without their faults and problems. Life gives all of us continual challenges. But overall—oh my! God has been so good, so faithful to me.

I've been stuck on the floor of despair, with a heart that said, "I can *not* get up again, Lord! I can't do this!"

But he won't let me stay on the floor. He says, "Thelma, of course you can't fly on your own. You have to soar on the wind of my Spirit. With my wind beneath those little wings of yours that are always flappin' in prayer, you will rise. Child, hold on. You and I, together, are about to fly above your circumstances."

Time and time and time again he has proven faithful when all seemed lost. In fact, I've learned to fly under so many impossible situations that I think I may now be qualified to be called a Queen Bee.

Do you feel as though you have fallen and simply cannot get up? Trust his power to change your life. Offer up a prayer of faith and believe your Father will take care of you and all of your concerns. Let go of the stuff that weighs you to earth. Embrace anything that lifts you higher. Soon you'll be off the dark ground of despair and buzzin' around in the fresh morning air.

* * *

God met me more than halfway, he freed me from my anxious fears. Look at him; give him your warmest smile. Never hide your feelings from him. When I was desperate, I called out, and God got me out of a tight spot.

Psalm 34:4–6 MSG

mystery shoppers

Bonnie Afman Emmorey

. . . .

The mystery of life isn't a problem to solve,
but a reality to experience.

FRANK HERBERT

*I*t was 1982. My son Nathan was two years old, and Jordan was an infant. Life should have been perfect, but I was starting to feel like a crazy woman. It felt like my life revolved around feeding babies, changing diapers, and doing laundry.

Thank goodness for Chris! We met two years earlier at a basketball game when our first sons were two weeks old. We connected! We were from vastly different backgrounds, but we shared kindred spirits. Chris and I spent hours on the phone discussing everything from current events to silent husbands. I believe she saved my sanity.

We would often meet at the local grocery store and, after running our respective errands, we would end up in the coffee shop where we would kick back, relax, and talk. Chris was highly creative, and we would often find ourselves trying to figure out what we could do at home to bring in extra money as stay-at-home moms.

As we lingered over coffee one afternoon, a vice president of the grocery store chain sat down with us to chat. We both knew him through our church, but his job offer took us completely by surprise. He was developing a new program for store evaluation and wondered if we'd be interested in part-time employment.

He wanted to hire us, two *obvious* housewives, to become "mystery shoppers." The grocery store chain would give us money, send us to their stores all over northern Michigan, let us shop, and *pay us* for evaluating the efficiency of the store employees. It was every woman's dream job — being *paid* to shop! The fact that we had to give everything back didn't bother us a bit. I have always considered shopping to be my best sport, so this appeared to be a perfect match.

Chris and I set off on our first day filled with high expectations of great fun — but some surprises were in store for me. As a part of our job description, we were asked to be rude to sales clerks, to try to use expired coupons, and to sneak items out of the stores on the bottom rack of the shopping carts — without paying for them. Obviously, our *real* job was to write up reports following the store visits on how well the employees were doing with catching crooks.

At the end of our first day, I went home exhausted from the stress of being so deceptive and dishonest. I'd never done anything like this before in my life. Chris was having a blast, but I told my husband I didn't think I could continue. It was too difficult. Ron reminded me I had made a commitment and I should follow through with the assignment.

I went back to work anticipating another difficult experience, but was surprised to discover by the third day, I was having a ball seeing how much I could get away with at each store. And I was *good* at it!

The following Sunday morning we were studying James 1:27 NKJV: "Pure and undefiled religion before God and the Father is this: . . . to keep oneself unspotted from the world."

An alarm went off in my head. I could see exactly what happened. I had been hired to do a job that, if I had been doing it for any other reason, would have been morally and legally wrong. Yes, at first I had found it difficult, and I was tempted to quit, but the more I did it, the easier it became. I even *enjoyed* it! I had allowed myself to touch the world, and my perspective had been altered. What a lesson! Chris and I had been having so much fun, we almost missed the important lesson that what we were doing demanded personal integrity and accountability — to God and to each other.

Over the next few years, Chris and I continued to be "mystery shoppers," even resorting to simple disguises if we thought anyone in the stores might recognize us. It gave us time away from the routine of kids, husbands, and housework, produced needed income, and was great fun. But I had a new perspective. God *would* hold me accountable, and I'd better guard my heart regarding matters of personal integrity.

. . . .

Real religion, the kind that passes muster before
God the Father, is this: . . . guard against corruption
from the godless world.

JAMES 1:27 MSG

binkies, baggage, and the billion-dollar question

Sandi Banks

Our love for people and our hope in Christ will put us in a position to point to Christ when asked about it.

John Fischer

I stepped off the airplane with baby Laura in my arms. Grandpa met us at the gate and offered to hold her while I went downstairs to the baggage claim area. I stood alone, waiting for my bags — just me — and holding the baby's Binkie pacifier. A flight attendant began staring, first at me, then at the pacifier, then back at me. Finally she leaned over and whispered, "Excuse me, miss. Is this your first flight?"

Actually, issuing pacifiers to airline passengers who need them is not such a bad idea. Those folks are easy to spot. Their hands clutch the armrests, their eyes stare at the airsick bag, and both sides of their brain argue over who gets to sit nearest the exit as the plane picks up speed along the runway. My heart goes out to those with a deathly fear of flying. Moreover, it goes out to those who have had that fear — and sat next to *me*.

Rather quickly, as a seasoned flyer, I discern their plight. If I sense the least bit of receptivity, I try to help them during take-off by distracting them or convincing them that airplanes are, indeed, the safest way to fly. If that doesn't work, I attempt to comfort them with up-to-date research on jet propulsion and physics facts that explain how the thrust, lift, drag, and weight properties make it nearly impossible for the plane *not* to fly. No one has ever requested to sit by me a second time. So much for trying to be helpful!

I'll never forget the flight where I settled into the window seat with my Bible, my journal, and a prayer that went something like this: "O Lord, this is *my* time with y*o*u. Please don't put anyone in this row — just you and me, Lord, all the way, okay?"

Sanctimoniously, I buckled in and opened to the Psalms. In the periphery, I noticed someone putting a bag into the overhead compartment and settling into the seat beside me. Curtly, I muttered under my breath, "Lord, I thought we had a deal — this is a mistake!"

Then I heard a soft, quivering voice. "Aren't you *scared* to fly?"

Instead of immediately dispensing my usual "helpful hints," I was overcome with compassion for this young Filipino girl whose name, I soon learned, was Miriam. Her question led straight into my own faith story.

"Actually, Miriam, I used to be petrified of flying. I had an awful fear of death."

"And you aren't scared anymore? Wow, *what happened?*"

The "billion-dollar question."

I began simply to share how I dreaded every Easter as a child and was probably the only kid in Denver to shed sad tears into her Easter basket. "Though my 'outside' was festive, with bonnets and new patent leather shoes, my 'inside' was a different story." I told her how I'd listen to the Easter message in church and stress over Jesus' death so much that I would mentally shut down before hearing the wonderful part about his resurrection.

"I was so focused on the *bad* news that I never heard the *good* news! Then one day I learned I could have a personal relationship with the risen Lord and I no longer needed to fear death, but could actually look forward to spending eternity with him!"

The conversation took an exciting, life-changing turn as God began doing his miraculous work in this young woman's heart. The plane landed. After we disembarked, Miriam eagerly gathered her entire family together, glanced in my direction, and said, "Now tell them everything you told me!"

So in the course of my ten-minute layover, I shared my best *Reader's Digest* version of the gospel message before reboarding the airplane.

I thought back to my pious prayer request for uninterrupted time with the Lord. Thankfully, he overruled.

Our disappointments and our interruptions are often divine appointments. I wonder how many opportunities I've missed because my own agenda got in the way. I'm learning that God has a grand purpose and a plan for me every day. Sometimes it involves putting my own scheduled activity aside, no matter how admirable it seems, in order to follow his agenda for my day.

At any moment, someone may ask me the "billion-dollar question." I hope I never miss an opportunity to give the "price-less answer."

Always be prepared to give an answer to everyone who asks you to give the reason for the hope that you have.

1 PETER 3:15

the color of love

Thelma Wells

God loves you simply because he has chosen to do so. He loves you when you don't feel lovely. He loves you when no one else loves you. Others may abandon you, divorce you and ignore you. But God will love you. Always. No matter what.

MAX LUCADO

*I*t wasn't so long ago that I had to go around to the back door of a restaurant to order a hamburger just because my skin wasn't white. And there I stood, next to the garbage dumpster in the alley, waiting for my order.

As an ambitious young lady just out of high school and attempting to register at a secretarial school, I was so excited! I dressed up in my pretty blue dress and topped it all with my blue high heel shoes and pretty blue bag, confident that I could make a good impression and attend that school. But within minutes my young heart was crushed. Because of the color of my skin, I was unceremoniously escorted out of the office before I could even register.

It would have been easy to let one hurt pile upon another, and I have only shared two brief experiences of prejudice here. Imagine what the average black person my age has endured. Contemplate the assault to their very personhood, and all based on the shade of their skin pigment.

It was tempting to flash my own weapons of anger and fight evil with evil, but as a Christian, I read that the apostle Paul explained, "For God is pleased with you when, for the sake of your conscience, you patiently endure unfair treatment. Of course, you get no credit for being patient if you are beaten for doing wrong. But if you suffer for doing right and are patient beneath the blows, God is pleased with you" (1 Peter 2:19–20 NLT).

When I had to drink out of a water fountain labeled "Colored" because I might contaminate the water for white folks, was that kind of outrageous injustice okay? Did God just want me and other black folks to take it? Dr. Martin Luther King Jr. didn't think so. I don't think so. But one thing I have learned through the years: we are free to hate, but as Christians wouldn't it be more fitting to use our freedom to love?

Love is patient, love is kind. . . . It is not rude, it is not self-seeking, it is not easily angered, it keeps no record of wrongs. Love does not delight in evil but rejoices with the truth. It always protects, always trusts, always hopes, always perseveres. Love never fails.

1 CORINTHIANS 13:4 – 8

an empowering choice

Cathy Gallagher

* *

*Cold words freeze people and hot words scorch them,
and bitter words make them bitter, and wrathful words
make them wrathful. Kind words produce their image
on men's souls — and a beautiful image it is.*

Pascal

When I answered the phone, I recognized his voice and thought I was prepared for anything. I was wrong. After hearing his request, I was tempted to say mean words to my former employer and then slam down the receiver. I thought: *You've got to be kidding! Why would I do this for you after what you did to me? The nerve!*

My mind flashed back to three weeks earlier when the same company president who was on the phone called me into his office and said, "Cathy, six weeks ago I hired you as customer service director. You get here early. You stay late. You're always upbeat and you have a positive attitude. You've done some good things while you've been here, but you don't fit my culture. I'm letting you go."

I don't fit your culture? Why not? What does that mean? I wondered. It didn't make sense. When he hired me the president had said, "Cathy, you have all the skills and experience I had hoped to find in someone; you are *exactly* the person I am looking for." A few weeks later, he fired me.

Now, on the phone, the company president was making a bold, nervy request: "Cathy, you are a good writer and your articles have been published. Will you write the story of my company and get it published in the industry journal I most want it to be in?"

My thoughts swirled: *This is amazing. You don't think I fit your culture, so you fired me. Now you want me to write for you! In your dreams! Why should I?*

I felt the same surge of hurtful anger on the phone I felt when I was being fired. I also felt the same urge to say unkind words. When he was firing me, however, I had forced myself to zip my lips and turn a favorite Bible verse into a silent prayer before I spoke. That prayer helped me get through that awful meeting with professional dignity.

On the phone, I zipped my lips and prayed the silent prayer I had prayed while being fired only three weeks earlier: "May the words of my mouth and the thoughts of my heart be pleasing to you, O Lord, my rock and my redeemer" (Psalm 19:14 NLT). Then I took a breath and humbly and quietly said, "Yes,

I'll write your story and get it published." I had no idea what would happen next.

Usually the publishing process takes many months, but not this time. I knew the journal and the types of stories the editor preferred. Several years earlier, at the editor's request, I had ghostwritten a story for this journal, so I felt comfortable presenting the story idea over the phone. The editor said she wanted the story if I could get it to her within a month. I assured her I could meet this deadline.

Writing the story involved interviewing the president. As the twenty-seven-year-old president told me the details of how he developed his business from a seed of an idea into a thriving six-million-dollar business in only eight years, I developed a new respect for him. I put aside my anger at being fired and focused on writing a story that would make us proud we had worked together.

Much to my delight and surprise, the editor gave the story the most prestigious spot in the tabloid-size journal — the center two-page spread. And she agreed to purchase a second story from me, which was published six months later.

The best part of this experience took place on the day I presented an advance copy of the journal to the company president. After he read the story, I asked if he liked it. His eyes danced when he said, "Oh, yes, Cathy. It is much more than I expected or ever dreamed possible."

It was more than I expected too. The money the president paid me for writing his story, after my tithe to my church, covered an entire month's worth of my living expenses, which was important, since I was unemployed.

When I think about the choice I made to pray that my words would be pleasing on the day the company president fired me, and again, three weeks later, when he made his request on the phone, I understood the relationship between my words and my life experiences. The words I choose to say either limit or expand my world — mean words limit, but kind words can expand my horizons by opening doors of opportunity.

. . . .

Be gracious in your speech. The goal is to bring out the best in others in a conversation, not put them down, not cut them out.

Colossians 4:6 MSG

defiant ways

Melissa S. Sutter

A Chinese philosopher said, "Parents who are afraid to put their foot down usually have children who step on toes."

14,000 QUIPS & QUOTES

Our 1972 Chevy Impala was built like a boat. There was plenty of room for my brother and me to sit on the floor behind the front seats. And, since there were no seat belt laws at that time, that was a favorite place for us to ride. As Mom took her place behind the wheel, she remembered something. "Kids, I left my purse in the house. I'll be right back."

The two minutes it was going to take for her to run in and get her purse was more than enough time for me, a "sweet" six-year-old girl, to develop a master plan and obtain the cooperation of Danny, my five-year-old brother.

As my mom entered the house and shut the door, I looked directly at my brother and seriously admitted, "I feel like swearing."

Since my parents did not swear, our swearing vocabulary was limited. However, like my mom always said, "If you set your mind to doing something, you can do it!" I started the naughty banter by calling my brother a couple words of which I was confident my mom and dad would have cringed and called "cuss words." That was all it took. Danny joined right in my fun little name-calling game by returning a sentence with his own nasty little words. Back and forth the swearing went as we laughed and laughed.

Suddenly, between giggles, we heard a familiar but sickening sound. It was the "Uh-hum" sound that only an angry mother can make. Yes! Our mom was standing outside the car and, unfortunately, the car window was down. She had been listening to our new little game and did not think it was nearly as funny as we did only a few seconds earlier.

How she managed to open a car door, grab both of us by the arms, and haul us through the house at such great speed, I will never know! It felt as though my feet were flapping behind me as my long hair blew in the wind. Instantly, it seemed, we were transported to the bathroom. I had no idea what the consequences were going to be for our misbehavior, but I was confident I wouldn't like it. Eyes open wide, lips sucked in, and hands covering our behinds, we waited for our sentencing.

Mom very calmly told us that swearing was not allowed, and that we would learn what soap tasted like as a reminder to keep our language clean. Being what Dr. Dobson would call a "strong-willed child," I thought this sounded more like a *challenge* than a *punishment*.

Holding the Dial soap up to Danny, Mom didn't have to say anything. In compliance, he licked the soap, made a wrinkly-nosed face, and sweetly apologized to Mom.

It was my turn. Not wanting her to think I was distressed with the punishment, I smiled as Mom held up the soap. Instead of licking the Dial, I determined it would be best to make my point by biting off an entire corner of the bar — which I did with great determination and vigor. Familiar with my defiant ways, Mom just let me chew. And chew. And chew. The soap did not taste good. As a matter of fact, it was intolerable. My mom noticed the color leaving my cheeks and knew I was about to lose my breakfast.

"Spit it out," she demanded.

Between gags I choked out, "No! I like it!"

More urgently this time, she pleaded, "Spit it out, Melissa Sue!"

"No, it's good," I insisted as the golden suds began to escape my mouth.

"Melissa!" It was too late for her request. I suppressed a final gag and proceeded to redecorate our bathroom.

I'm not sure which of us learned the greater lesson that day. I quit swearing. My mom never made me eat soap again. Of course, I was only six years old and I had many more lessons to learn.

Thinking back over my behavior in front of Danny that day, I wonder:

How many times have I set a poor example?

How often have I been gagging on something nasty in my life, insisting I like it?

How many times has God tried to correct me, teach me, or lead me, only to have me spit the lesson out because of my stubborn ways?

. . . .

For people who hate discipline and only get more stubborn, there'll come a day when life tumbles in and they break, but by then it'll be too late to help them.

PROVERBS 29:1 MSG

my front porch family

Thelma Wells

. . . .

*There it was: the faith, the encouragement, these strands
of reassurance woven into a network of mutual support.
Nobody had to face anything without allies whose loyalty
was beyond question. Nobody was ever alone.*

ARTHUR GORDON

*T*hough I wouldn't wish the days of segregation on anyone, perhaps the one blessing in this period of history was that in small black communities, we looked out for each other with an urgent watchfulness. In my neighborhood, if you didn't know what you were doing, Honey, you can be sure somebody else did.

I'll never forget the day I was about nine years old and walking down the street in my pretty ruffled dress feeling as safe as a little chick in a coop of friendly folks who cared about me. Then a sleek black Cadillac, with longhorns on its hood, slowly pulled up alongside me. The driver leaned across the seat to roll down the window and offer me a ride. I glanced at him, curious, but kept walking. At this point, he stopped the car and said, "Hey, little girl, come here."

Shrugging, I took a step toward the car and leaned on the door to look inside. But before I could say a word, I heard a shriek that rattled the street.

Althea Hilliard (a friend of my family) had observed the scene from the dental office where she worked as a hygienist and rushed out the door. She was now hurtling herself toward me like a wild, mad hen on a mission.

"You get yourself away from here, girl!" Frantically, she waved her arms in my direction, shooing off invading forces of evil in our midst. When Althea finally reached me she took hold of my arms, squeezing them in a vice-like grip until we were eyeball to eyeball, nose to nose. "And don't you ever let me see you hangin' on this car or talkin' to this man again, you hear? Not this man or any other man, understand?"

All I could manage, with fear rising in my eyes and pain throbbing in my arms, was a tremulous, "Yes, ma'am."

Then Althea turned to the man in the car and let loose on him the way only a furious hen — or an angry black mama — can. If Althea had not been watching out for me, who knows what might have happened to me and my girlhood innocence that afternoon?

The men of our neighborhood were equally protective. If I dawdled on the way home and passed Mr. Bodden's shoe shop later than usual, he greeted me with a frown and a scolding.

"School's been out for a half an hour, little girl," he'd say, nodding toward the clock on his shop wall. "You go on, now. I'm going to stand here and watch 'til you get home."

The eyes of my neighborhood were ever upon me — watching, observing, caring.

I don't think I grasped the value of this until I was an adult and realized my life was lived in front of a community that valued its children. I can't help but wonder what a difference it would make if every young person today could know they have "Someone to Watch Over Me." And not just *one* someone, but a *bunch* of someones.

For, indeed, it takes a front porch village of mamas, daddies, aunts, uncles, ministers, teachers, shop owners, and, yes, dental hygienists to raise children in the way they should go.

....

My eyes will watch over them for their good.

JEREMIAH 24:6

go, granny, go!

Gracie Malone

....

If only we could go back to the time when mistakes could be corrected by simply exclaiming, "Do over!"

UNKNOWN

I'd picked my five-year-old grandson Luke up after school, buckled him snugly in the back of my car, and was heading toward home when I rounded a curve a bit too fast. When my car swerved, he slapped his hand on his forehead and groaned, "Grandma Gracie, slow down. Don't you know curves are dangerous?" Before I could even apologize, he added, "I'd hate for anything to happen to you."

Of course, Luke was right! I made a vow right then and there to never speed when one of my grandchildren occupied the backseat of my car. Unfortunately, when alone, my mind sometimes drifts into midlife Netherlands, old habits take over, and I get going a bit too fast.

It was after such an occasion recently that I called our son Jason — the one I can usually count on to be sensitive and understanding. "Son," I began sweetly, "could you explain what 'deferred adjudication' means?"

Instead of giving me a straightforward answer, my bright young college student burst out laughing and asked, "How many speeding tickets have you gotten, Mom?"

"Just two," I whined, "but they were biggies — one in a school zone, of all things, and the other, well . . . in a construction zone."

"Mom, what were you thinking?"

"Sometimes my mind wanders! Anyway, I've already taken care of the school zone offense by taking defensive driving online. But now . . . well . . ." I took a deep breath and continued, "I was running late for a hair appointment and didn't even notice the guys placing orange cones on the road until, that is, I saw a motorcycle cop do a U-ey and flash his red and blue lights. As I pulled onto the shoulder, I couldn't help but notice the officer's fine leather jacket and black, shiny boots, so I ran my fingers through my hair, pasted on my best smile, and lowered the window to say good morning."

"Mom, you didn't try to charm him out of a ticket, did you?" Jason asked.

"Well . . . not exactly . . ."

For the next few minutes, I gave just enough detail to incur Jason's sympathy and get the information I needed. After I hung up, my mind returned to the scene of the crime. I *did not* try to charm the officer, but while I was fumbling for my driver's license, I *did* decide to get something off my chest.

"Sir," I began in a matter-of-fact tone, "may I say just one thing?"

"Sure, ma'am."

"Well . . ." I smoothed the wrinkles in my skirt, sucked in a huge gulp of air, and said, "The cars in front of me were driving the same speed I was."

The officer shook his head, grinned, and said, "I know that, Lady, but I can only catch you people one at a time." He handed over the citation, turned on his well-polished heels, and remounted his bike.

I slipped my car in gear and proceeded — very slowly — down the road toward the beauty shop. A few days later I appeared in court, ready to ask for deferred adjudication.

The judge peered over her glasses as she addressed the group of malefactors — who, I might add were mostly *young* and *male* — seated in the courtroom. "Don't even think about not telling the truth," she began, "because we have records of every offense you've committed in the state of Texas." She cleared her throat and added, "Speak up when you address the court."

My heart pounded as I waited my turn.

When the bailiff finally called my name, I stepped to the bench and, speaking fast and a bit too loud, rattled off the four driving violations — only *four*, mind you — of my entire life, including one for an out-of-date inspection sticker.

The judge was not impressed with my record or with my honesty. "Probation for one hundred twenty days!" she declared. Then she pointed her bony finger at me and added, "We'll be watching you!"

As I paid my fine and headed out the door, I felt like a real criminal. Throughout the next four months I had to deal with my misgivings: *How could I, a protective mother and doting grandmother who'd preached caution to her offspring, end up a reckless speed demon on wheels?* I also endured unmerciful teasing from the men in our family. It began as soon as I got home from court when I called Jason and asked, "Now, what does probation mean?"

. . . .

Be a good citizen. All governments are under God.
Insofar as there is peace and order, it's God's order.
So live responsibly as a citizen. . . . Duly constituted authorities
are only a threat if you're trying to get by with something.
Decent citizens should have nothing to fear.

ROMANS 13:1, 3 MSG

battle of the ding dongs

Rachel St. John-Gilbert

· ·

If you lose the power to laugh, you lose the power to think.

CLARENCE DARROW

*A*n author friend graciously offered to review my manuscript for a book of humorous devotionals. Well versed in English and grammar, she was stumped by the word *Ding-Dong*, which I had chosen to hyphenate. Not finding it in her volume of *Hyphenated Words for the Hyperactive Hyphenator*, Lynn had a stroke of genius.

She called her husband, who was on his way to the grocery store. Newly health-conscious, Mike was on a mission in search of low-fat foods to prolong not only his life but that of his wife and their young daughter, Sheridan.

Phone in hand, Lynn was on the case. "Michael, dear, I'm so glad you've arrived at the store. I'm working on Rachel's book and need to know if Ding-Dongs are hyphenated."

Multitasking Michael, who was browsing the rice cake aisle with cell phone in hand, didn't hesitate. "Lynn, of course Ding

Dongs are hydrogenated — but it doesn't matter. I'm not buying any — Sheridan doesn't need to be eating that junk anyway."

Lynn and I had a good laugh — but the story doesn't stop there. We each began to sense the seed of a good story germinating. But *whose* story was it?

You've got to understand. I was raised in a family of wordsmith vultures, always circling the dinner table, coffee table, Ping-Pong table (you name it) looking for fodder for a chapter, an essay, or a blockbuster title. Whenever someone uttered funny or insightful material, we would scramble like puppies chasing the chuck wagon in search of a napkin and pen to jot down the literary morsel. If we couldn't find paper, we would write on our hands because the unwritten rule of thumb (so to speak) was that whoever wrote it down first got to use the goods.

Believe me, it gets pretty crazy with several writers in the hunt. We've even developed our own version of Miranda rights to read to our friends and relatives. Upon whipping out our pens to record that catchy phrase, wrap up that witticism, or capture the coveted laugh-out-loud funny, we warn: "Any slightly humorous, entertaining, or profound utterance from your mouth can and will be considered fair game for publication in one of our stories. But we promise not to use it against you!"

So back to poor Lynn. She too is a writing scavenger who can spot publishable prey a mile away, and, after all, it was *her* husband who unwittingly coughed up the cutie. Yet I really wanted to use the hydrogenated slipup in my own book. What to do with our Ding-Dong dilemma? Well, in the spirit of friendship, Lynn decided not to prolong the battle of the Ding Dongs. Instead, she consented to let me use the incident here and now as a gift to you — but only after I signed over the rights to my firstborn grandchild. Sheeze! It's brutal out there in Christian publishing.

And is Ding Dong hyphenated? As you see in this story, sometimes yes, sometimes no. Just don't ask me to explain when! Go ask your grammar teacher.

Would that we pursued the things of God with the single-minded focus of writers desperate for good material. Would that we treasured Scripture, reveled in the power of prayer, and immersed ourselves in the joy of sharing Christ's love with others. Perhaps we should write our own Miranda rights: Anything *God* says can and will be used to make me all that I was created to be — to the glory of God and the blessing of those around me.

* * *

*It's in Christ that we find out who we are
and what we are living for.*

EPHESIANS 1:11 MSG

two little words
made all the difference

Patricia Lorenz

....

*Opportunity . . . often it comes disguised in the form of
misfortune or temporary defeat.*

Napoleon Hill

A few years ago I helped some dear friends move from
their condo in Florida to a bigger home with three
bedrooms and an attached in-ground pool. The day
after the move they left me to house-sit for eight days while they
headed for a long-planned-for skiing vacation in Montana.

I was in heaven. The whole house to myself. A beautiful pool.
A bicycle. A lovely neighborhood near the intercoastal waterway
and less than a mile from the Gulf of Mexico. Shirley even said
I could drive her brand-new PT Cruiser if I wanted to. All week
I read, wrote, swam, biked, shopped, and relaxed to the max.

One morning I started out on a bike ride, being very careful on the mile-long stretch of busy road that had no sidewalks

or even much of a shoulder, for that matter. When I arrived at my shopping destination, I got off the bike and walked it carefully through a busy five-lane intersection. I admit I got into the intersection just as the walk signal changed and it did take me longer than normal to maneuver the heavy bike with my big bag and water bottle in the deep metal basket.

All of a sudden, *wham!* I was knocked to the ground by a car. A woman making a left turn ran right into me. I fell on top of the bike, and the basket came unhinged, spilling all my stuff into the street. Dazed, I tried to scramble up, but fell back down on the bike, terrified that the maze of traffic would run over me. Finally, I was able to stand up. My left leg and right ankle hurt like crazy, but I managed to gather the bike, bag, and basket and hobble out of the intersection.

I dropped the bike on the grass next to the sidewalk and tried to reattach the basket. I couldn't figure it out. Suddenly, I just stood there and the tears came. No one had stopped to help me. Even the woman who'd knocked me down had gone on. I didn't know a soul for miles, didn't know if I was really hurt or just in shock, and knew I couldn't ride home two miles carrying that big heavy bike basket under my arm.

I never felt more alone in my entire life. As cars whizzed by I stood there, scraped, bruised, confused, and scared.

Just then I looked up and saw a woman across the street standing next to her car waving her arms like a wild woman. When she got my attention, she motioned for me to meet her in the grocery store parking lot just a few feet from where I was standing. I nodded "okay" and gingerly inched my way to the blacktop.

"Oh, my dear, are you okay? I'm sorry! It was my fault. I didn't even look to the right. All I saw was that green arrow and I gunned it to make that left turn. Are you hurt? I have insurance. Do you need to go to the hospital?" She couldn't seem to stop talking long enough to hear my answers.

"No, I don't think I'm hurt. Just a few bruises and scrapes." At that moment the tears almost started up again and I could hardly talk.

"Are you sure you're okay? I'm so sorry. If the bike is damaged, I'll buy a new one. Honestly, I don't know what to say."

"Well," I stammered, "will you write down your name and phone number just in case?"

"Oh, yes, here, I have paper and pen in the car. My name's Beverly."

I explained, "I'm house-sitting for some friends who went to Montana and I don't know anyone around here. I was really upset that no one stopped to help me when I ended up flat down in the intersection. At least you stopped. I feel a lot better now. I thought it was a hit-and-run."

"Oh, goodness, no. I just didn't look before I turned. I am so sorry. Where are you from, my dear?"

"Wisconsin."

"Why, I'm from Wisconsin too! What town do you live in?"

"Milwaukee."

"Honey, I was born and raised in Milwaukee and lived there all my life until twenty years ago when we moved down here."

"My friends Wally and Shirley just moved into a new house over by St. Jerome's church. They're in the choir there."

"Would you believe that I'm the church housekeeper at St. Jerome's?"

Beverly and I were old chums by the time we parted. I figured out how to get the basket back on the bike, rode home, and within a week my bruises and scrapes were healed.

But most important, my feelings were healed as well. It's amazing how powerful two little words can be. Two little words from Beverly's mouth to my ears made all the difference, turning what could have been a highly stressful accident into somewhat of an adventure.

Two little words. "I'm sorry." And she meant it.

* *

Be kind to each other, tenderhearted, forgiving one another, just as God has forgiven you because you belong to Christ.

EPHESIANS 4:32 LB

morning smiles

Pauline Afman

. . . .

You can't deny laughter; when it comes, it plops down in your
favorite chair and stays as long as it wants.

STEPHEN KING

*J*t was a lazy morning and I stayed in bed long after I
awoke, enjoying the cool air coming in my bedroom
window. The doorbell rang and I heard my husband
open the front door. Evidently, a county work crew was cutting
off tree limbs along the road to ward off problems with electri-
cal lines. They requested permission to cut some branches off
the maple tree standing majestically on our front lawn.

Since I couldn't quite hear what was being said and was
feeling a bit nosy, I threw on my robe and peeked into the living room to see what was happening. Arriving just as the door
closed, I thought, "I got out of my warm bed for *this*?"

When my husband, Clyde, left to make his rounds at the
hospital and the nursing home as visitation pastor, I decided to

get comfortable in my living room lounge chair. Before long I snuggled under a soft cozy blanket and fell fast asleep.

The doorbell startled me out of a sound sleep. Glancing at the clock, I was amazed to discover an hour and a half had gone by since I sat down in my recliner. I wasn't even dressed! But someone was definitely at the door, and they weren't leaving.

Oh, well, my robe was more like a housedress and completely covered me, so I opened the door. There stood a handsome young man, one of the workers on the tree-trimming crew. He just wanted to verify that it was all right to cut off some of the limbs on the maple tree. I assured him it was fine. The young man had the oddest look on his face — quizzical? No, more like *amused*!

I hurried to the bathroom and looked in the mirror. My scant hair was standing straight up. I looked like a grandma sporting a very unattractive spike! What would my style-conscious grandsons think if they saw me now? I grinned at myself, thinking, *I now know why that young man was chuckling.*

A moment later, however, I discovered the *real* reason for his amusement. I had forgotten to put in my false teeth. Horrors! With my gums grinning back at me, I thought, *Appearance might not be everything, but in this case, it's quite a bit!* I blushed like a young girl and laughed out loud.

Fortunately, at my advanced age of eighty-one, there aren't many people I still feel the need to impress. I know outward beauty is fleeting, but I think I'll make it a priority to look in the mirror *before* I answer the door anytime soon. After all, it might be one of my cute grandsons!

. . . .

What matters is not your outer appearance — the styling of your hair, the jewelry you wear, the cut of your clothes — but your inner disposition. Cultivate inner beauty, the gentle, gracious kind that God delights in.

1 Peter 3:3 – 4 MSG

sisters of the heart

Carol Kent

. . . .

There is a net of love by which you can catch souls.

MOTHER TERESA

*T*he invitation was unexpected. I had been asked to travel to Frankfurt, Germany, to speak for the five-day Worship and Study Conference sponsored by the PWOC (Protestant Women of the Chapel). The group was comprised of more than five hundred military wives and some active-duty military women from the fifty-five U.S. bases all over Europe. After landing in Frankfurt, my husband and I were driven to a picturesque ski resort town where the event was being held in a lovely hotel.

There was excitement in the air. I was immediately struck by the strong sense of sisterhood these women had with each other. Most were in their twenties or early thirties. For many, it was their first time living away from home in a foreign country, far from their mothers and their biological sisters. Many had husbands on deployment in Bosnia or Kosovo, and they felt alone in an unfamiliar environment — *except for the presence of their military sisters*. They explained to me that when you are in the military, you get close to each other very quickly because you get moved often — frequently every two years — and there is a strong bonding with other women who are in like circumstances.

My assignment was to speak every morning for the keynote sessions during the conference, and I also did a workshop on sharing your faith. When I came to the part about praying the prayer to become a Christian, I noticed several blank stares. Spontaneously I said, "Perhaps some of you have never invited Jesus to be your Savior and you would like to make that choice today." That day *seven* of those young military wives prayed and became Christians.

The following day I was walking down the hall toward my room in the hotel when I heard a voice behind me calling, "Carol, Heather wants to become a Christian, but we're not sure we can remember all of the words of that prayer. Can you come quickly and help us explain how she can ask Jesus into her life?"

I pivoted on my heel and followed my new friend down the hall. When we got to the hotel room, a whole group of women were already gathered there, eager to see Heather become a Christian. I looked at Heather. She had long brunette hair and it appeared she had not had much sleep. She was smoking with vigor, and I could tell the tension of this situation was causing her some stress.

I said, "Why don't we all gather in this room and begin by having some of you share how you became Christians?"

A lovely young woman next to me immediately put her hand in the air. "I'll go first," she said. "I went to church my whole life and I have always been a very good person. But it wasn't until I came to this conference that I found out you have to make it personal. I just became a Christian one hour ago!"

I was fighting back tears. The one-hour-old believer had given the first testimony in the group. One by one the rest of these women shared with honesty and authenticity what their lives had been like "before Christ" and the difference he had made since they came to know him personally. It was a holy moment, and a hush fell on the room.

After pausing a moment, I looked at Heather and said, "You've heard some pretty amazing stories today." I went on. "It's very simple, but sometimes people try to make it complicated. The Bible teaches that God sent his Son, Jesus, to this earth. He was sinless and perfect. He grew to maturity and went into his public teaching ministry at the age of thirty. The religious leaders of the day didn't recognize him as the Savior of the world. They mocked him and ridiculed him. At age thirty-three he went through the most painful death invented by mankind — death by crucifixion. Jesus hung on a cross and paid the price for all of the wrongdoing in the world — my sin and yours. But the story doesn't end there. He rose again and he's in heaven today preparing a place for those who believe."

I concluded, "Heather, I don't think it was an accident that you were invited to this conference. God knew you needed to find him in the middle of all that's happening in your life. Are you interested in following me in a prayer to invite Christ into your life right now?"

Heather took one final drag on her cigarette and vigorously nodded her head. Everyone in the room stood in a circle, and this sisterhood of military women looped their arms around each other. Heather began to pray, confessing her sin and inviting Jesus Christ to be her Savior and Lord. She prayed right out loud with no embarrassment and no hesitation.

There were no dry eyes in the room. As the prayer ended, Susan, the woman who had invited Heather to the conference, wrapped her arms around her friend and gently rocked her back and forth as she sang a song of welcome into the body of Christ.

I hugged Heather and Susan and asked, "How did the two of you meet?"

Susan smiled. "We both have daughters named Harley."

I found myself chuckling, thinking only motorcycle people would name a baby girl Harley. But God had a different idea. The story unfolded. Heather and Susan were in the military commissary at the same time when Susan called her daughter, "H-a-r-l-e-y!" Heather wondered who was calling her daughter, and the two women met. But they had *nothing* in common. Susan was deeply involved in her Christian faith and Heather wasn't interested.

Time passed and God put on the heart of Susan to invite Heather to the conference. Heather's husband had been deployed, and she was lonely and fearful. Susan displayed a love and concern for Heather that drew her to accept the invitation. And that's how two military wives became sisters in Christ at a hotel in Germany.

. . . .

God didn't go to all the trouble of sending his Son merely to point an accusing finger, telling the world how bad it was. He came to help, to put the world right again. Anyone who trusts in him is acquitted.

JOHN 3:17–18 MSG

the birdcage christmas tree

Ginger Shaw

· ·

Attitudes are the quiet judgments that shape our lives; they mold the form that living takes.

FOUND IN A CHURCH BULLETIN

J stood there staring. What was that thing hanging from the stairs above the atrium? Black wrought iron covered with a gold garland, shiny colored ornaments hanging around the edges, and filled with small, wrapped packages. I looked at my sister. She rolled her eyes and shrugged. I looked at my mother. Her eyes shone brightly as she said, "It's a Christmas tree!"

Oh, yeah. Right. A Christmas tree? Well, it *was* Christmas Eve. We had just returned from a midnight church service. But it didn't feel like Christmas. And this certainly didn't look like a tree. Two feet high, black metal? What a pathetic tree!

Our holidays had always been different by most standards. We moved so often we seldom knew where we would be or what to expect. But we always had our immediate family — my dad, mother, two sisters, and me. And we always had a fresh, green Christmas tree. Our small family holidays were precious times to each of us.

But this year we had just arrived in Bangkok, Thailand — not exactly your winter wonderland. My dad was on a mission with the Air Force, flying out of Laos and unable to come home for the holidays. My older sister was in college in the States. What little extended family we had was scattered across the U.S. Even our dog was lost in transit and wouldn't arrive for several days. So there we stood — my mother, my younger sister, and me. Alone. Christmas Eve. In a Buddhist country on the far side of the world. No friends. No dog. No Christmas fun. Part of the family was missing. What a pathetic holiday!

My gaze returned to the "tree." I wondered what my mother was thinking. Had the heat gotten to her? Had she contracted some exotic disease? Had she just gone crazy?

She tried to explain. "Evergreen trees don't grow on this tropical land. They're not imported because Buddhists have no need of Christmas trees." She told us the artificial trees, received at the military commissary in July, were purchased quickly by the savvy families who had probably endured a treeless Christmas the year before.

So my resourceful mother decided to create her own version of a Christmas tree. Mother has always loved wrought iron, and in Bangkok you could have it made to order. I thought perhaps this was just an excuse to add more of it to her collection. But she insisted it was her Christmas spirit that prompted her to design this birdcage to hang beneath the stairs in our temporary home. She dug through the unpacked boxes to find our decorations and hung the newly wrought birdcage above the indoor atrium. Finally she filled the inside with small brightly wrapped boxes. Notice I said *boxes*, not gifts. The one moment of excitement at the sight of all the presents faded quickly as Mother told us they were just for decoration. What a pathetic holiday!

That was the first Christmas our family wasn't together. I'd like to say we were like the family in *Little Women*, thankful and joyful for our little birdcage Christmas tree, gathered around the atrium singing carols — but my memory tells me otherwise.

Looking back, I know it wasn't an easy holiday for my mother, and I know my attitude didn't make it any easier. But her determination to make the best of all circumstances, wherever, and with whatever God provided, is a reflection of her attitude in life today. And it made her a *great* military wife. I've seen it through countless changes — moves, illness, and widowhood.

I don't remember many of the presents I've received over the years, but I *do* remember the gift of the birdcage Christmas tree. And today it hangs in my office to remind me not of that pathetic holiday, but of the priceless gift Mother passed on to me — a positive attitude!

....

Be cheerful no matter what; pray all the time; thank God no matter what happens. This is the way God wants you who belong to Christ Jesus to live.

1 Thessalonians 5:16–18 MSG

late bloomer

Jeanne Doyon

"Oh, how happy I am!" the little kite cried,
"And all because I was brave, and tried."

"How the Little Kite Learned to Fly,"
William J. Bennett, *The Book of Virtues*

J glanced at my costume hanging on the hook, and my stomach fluttered. My fun idea now seemed ludicrous. What possessed me to take dance lessons? Lessons were one thing, but going on stage was quite another. I paced, sipping water to help my nerve-induced dry mouth. *Jitters are normal*, I reminded myself.

Dancing was in my blood — at least it was something I had to get out of my system. All my life I longed to take lessons, and now, at thirty-nine years old, I had decided to try. My mom and her sister danced in many recitals and competitions while

76

growing up. My grandmother, Memere, sewed costumes till her eyes glazed over, putting sequins on by hand. My mother eventually went on to be a dance instructor and, even after giving birth to me, continued teaching. It was perfectly natural for her to enroll me in classes when I turned two.

On the night of my dance recital, however, I wouldn't go on stage. My mother was frantic with backstage arrangements and getting the dance numbers ready on time. My dad was running the lights and manning the curtains. They both tried to get me to participate in the program with the rest of the members of the class, but no amount of encouragement or coercing could persuade me to change my mind. There was no way I was walking out on that platform.

In desperation, my dad said to me, "If you don't go out on that stage, you will never take dance lessons again."

We have all done it. As parents, we make a threat and then must follow through. My dad was good to his word, and I never took dance lessons again as a child. I don't remember much about that night, but remnants of fear remain — unexplained tears, feelings of choking suffocation when the music is played, and a memory of floral bouquets.

. . . .

Well, you're going on stage tonight, I thought. At that moment my grandmother's little blue Escort pulled into the driveway. The old fearfulness in me rose and I wanted to run.

"Jeannie!" Memere squealed with an excitement not normally demonstrated. "I know you'll be wonderful."

We arrived at the auditorium about twenty minutes later and Memere could hardly contain her excitement. As soon as we entered, her feet started tapping to the music already playing. The music only made the panic rise higher in my chest.

"You'll do fine," she said, beaming from ear to ear. "I've been waiting thirty-seven years for this." I bent down, kissed her wrinkled cheek, and headed for the dressing room.

"Break a leg!" she shouted. My grandmother and my mom didn't know I had placed a line in the program that read:

"Better late than never! Love, Jeanne"

Even if I was scared witless or got stage fright, I needed to do this. Fear had held me captive for too long. I was missing life. As I approached forty, I was attempting things I never dreamed I could do — and it was fun! God had begun a work in me and I was learning that perfect love *does* cast out fear.

The theme from *Alice in Wonderland* began, and from backstage I heard the applause. My stomach churned as the time for our number approached. Standing in the darkened wings backstage, my heart thumped as I tried to remember the routine we had practiced over and over. My dance partners whispered in my ear and encouraged me as I prayed for the strength to finally dance the way I had always dreamed.

"This is for you," I whispered, thinking of Mom and Memere. The music started and my partners and I arrived on stage, right on cue. I danced my heart out and found myself having the time of my life. I may have been thirty-seven years late, but I finally did it, and it felt good.

I found out later that Memere's heart danced right along with mine from her seat in the audience. For her to see her oldest granddaughter on stage was a dream come true. For me, the dance represented much more. I felt the Lord release the chains that had held me in captivity for more than three decades. That evening represented a new beginning of embracing life with exuberance, freedom, and joy.

I can do everything through him who gives me strength.

PHILIPPIANS 4:13

the "planned" pregnancy

Ginger Garrett

● ●

With God in charge, I believe everything will work out
for the best in the end.

HENRY FORD

I had the most perfect birthing plan in modern history. Because I had struggled with infertility and three miscarriages, I wanted this birth to be incredibly special. (As it turns out, so did God, but we had very different ideas about how to get that done.) I had carefully planned everything, including choosing the perfect midwife and scheduling my induction of labor on the perfect day.

So at five o'clock on a Monday morning, I was showered, packed, and ready to roll (literally) to the hospital. The problem was, suddenly no bed was available. Atlanta had been hit with "maternity mania" and everyone in the city was delivering at once. Because my induction time was scheduled, I was low priority. The nurse who phoned encouraged me to fib, to say I was bleeding or in labor so I could move up the priority list, but I didn't feel comfortable doing that. So I waited.

"It will only be a few hours," she reassured me. "But try not to eat, in case we need to do a C-section."

My husband had taken off work and my mother had flown in from Texas. My in-laws were on standby. Everyone was ready for the baby to be born — except the baby and the hospital. So we languished around the house, none of us able to concentrate on television or reading. Everyone kept stealing furtive, hopeful glances at my bulging tummy, hoping against hope the baby would make a sudden dash for the end zone, a "Hail Mary pass" of labor and delivery.

I was the proverbial watched pot, and I wasn't boiling. And now I was hungry and cranky too. My sister-in-law, Stephanie, who is a natural childbirth instructor, didn't understand why I had to plan every detail.

"Birthing is a beautiful process, and it should be as natural as possible," she coaxed me.

"I got a French manicure," I insisted. "That's as natural as I'm getting." (I couldn't leave something as monumental as birth to the whims of my uterus. That's what women did in the days before we had Palm Pilots.)

I was sorely testing everyone's patience. And the hospital was determined to test mine. There were no rooms available at five a.m. None at nine a.m. None at noon, and as the afternoon shadows stretched out, it didn't look good for a dinnertime delivery either. I didn't *want* a room after five p.m. because that would put me on a schedule of delivering around eight p.m., which meant I wouldn't get settled into my recovery suite until ten p.m., which was too late to be refreshed for receiving visitors the next morning.

So the next day, we started all over again. And once more, there were no rooms available. I couldn't believe it! All my careful plans, my thoughtful selection of a midwife (who was now off duty), my flowchart of traffic patterns on the interstates, even my ascertaining when the hospital got their delivery of fresh produce — out the window.

Hours later, we were finally told the hospital was ready for me. After I had been corralled into a bed and tagged with an identification band like a water buffalo on *Animal Planet*, it was time to begin the induction. I realized then what all my planning had been for: to avoid this cold fear of the unknown. Would I be a good mother for this little one? Would the baby ever sleep? Would I ever see my feet again? I was frightened and had been for nine months. My heart cried out silently to God.

Just then, the door swung open and I heard a friendly voice shout my name. It was Ginny, my infertility nurse. She had left the infertility clinic and had gone to work as a labor and delivery nurse. Out of the unusually large number of moms in the hospital that day, she had been "randomly" assigned to my room.

So the woman who had comforted me while I had miscarried or failed in another fertility cycle was the same woman cheering me on as I sweated and pushed. The woman who had called me so often to tell me I wasn't pregnant (again) was the same one who got to say, "It's a girl!"

All of my plans couldn't have brought me a delivery as sweet and profound as this one. God had upset my apple cart to remind me I was still the apple of his eye, even when I was uptight, bloated, and frightened. And I learned an important lesson: nothing I plan for myself can ever be better than what he has in store for me.

* * *

We humans keep brainstorming options and plans,
but God's purpose prevails.

PROVERBS 19:21 MSG

in-flight friendship

Charlotte Adelsperger

. . . .

Be kind. Remember everyone you meet is fighting a hard battle.

T. H. THOMPSON

*W*hen our plane took off from Kansas City for Newark, my heart pounded with excitement. *Tomorrow — Germany!* My husband Bob squeezed my hand. I ignored the young woman seated next to me who wore sunglasses and, obviously, wanted to be left alone.

After the usual airline snack, I flipped open a notebook full of German phrases.

"Looks like you're studying German," my seatmate said, peering over darkened lenses.

"Right." Then I told about our trip and how I was brushing up for my visit with a German friend who lived near Frankfurt.

"I studied in Frankfurt for three years," she said enthusiastically. She told me she was from Kenya, Africa, and was on her way home.

"Could you help me with my German?" I asked.

She did just that and she was a natural! We both launched into guttural sounds, smiles, and chuckles.

The humor of it all struck me. *Here I am flying across the country, learning German words from a young woman who is from Africa!*

I asked her name. "Caroline," she said, then her voice turned serious. "You've helped me more than you know. You see, when I got on the plane, I couldn't stop crying. You got my mind on other things." She explained how hard it was to leave both her brother and her sister who remained in the States.

Caroline asked me about values in American culture, and I discovered we were both Christians. I could tell she was well educated with strong faith in God. On the lighter side, we discovered we both love to play tennis. Caroline was young enough to be my daughter, but we seemed to connect on every topic.

While our plane descended, Caroline pulled out a business card. She explained it was from an American gentleman who had visited Kenya. "Do you know anything about this group?" she asked, pointing to the logo.

"That's a Christian organization I know well! I write for its magazines. This is amazing!" Quickly we shared our experiences.

Soon our plane landed in Newark. While we waited for our connecting flights, Bob and I enjoyed our time with Carolyn and treated her to her first root beer float.

"This is so good!" she said between sips. "Why didn't my brother or sister ever tell me about these?" she said with a chuckle. Yet her eyes still glimmered with a shadow of sadness.

When she and I stopped in the ladies' restroom, no one else was there. I noticed Caroline washing her hands at the far end of the long rectangular room.

All of a sudden a playful spirit swept over me, and in pantomime, I "hit" a tennis ball the length of the room to her. She pivoted to the right position and, with an extended arm, returned the imaginary shot. We broke into laughter. Back and forth we swung our invisible rackets. When I jumped for a high shot, a traveler walked in. She froze, speechless.

What a sight — two women from different generations, races, and nationalities swinging at each other and jumping around on the tile floor of a public restroom!

Before going to our separate gates, Caroline and I exchanged addresses. I hated to leave her — my delightful new friend. We hugged and promised to pray for each other.

When we returned from Europe, Caroline emailed: "I'm really excited that you have written to me. I thank the Lord for putting you in my path. You encourage me so much and you make me actually believe that life is all about people. You made my flight from America all the more bearable."

I was touched by her words and felt privileged to know her. We wrote often and shared prayer requests and dreams.

To my surprise, a year later Caroline flew to America with her father, Joseph, to attend her sister Agatha's college graduation.

During the Christmas holidays, all three of them were able to see us in Kansas City. At our home we savored our time together and sipped tea from Kenya. After dinner we took in the Christmas lights. My heart sang when I discovered more about our guests' close walk with the Lord.

After the holidays Caroline wrote, "You both are really like part of my family now. You have become more special to me as the days have gone by." That spirit continues in both of us.

I thought back to that joyful evening with Caroline and her family. At the end of our time together, she asked us to join in prayer. Words flowed in thanksgiving to God, and in my spirit I was again lifted in flight.

* * *

If I ride the wings of the morning, if I dwell by the farthest oceans, even there your hand will guide me, and your strength will support me.

PSALM 139:9–10 NLT

dancing queen

Debi Stack

. . . .

"Dance like no one's watching; love like you've never been hurt."

Unknown

*T*hree things made 1968 a great year for me: *Scooby-Doo* premiered on Saturday morning television, Elvis Presley's "In the Ghetto" debuted on the radio, and Tammy became my very best friend in third grade. During one of our frequent sleepovers, I'd had enough lighthearted giggling and swapping copies of *Tiger Beat* magazine.

"Hey, Tammy," I said, "let's play that new Elvis song on your record player — the one about the poor baby who grows up to have another poor baby and then dies."

"Why? It just makes you cry. Let's dance to 'Sugar, Sugar' by The Archies instead."

Tammy obviously didn't understand the melancholy temperament of a budding literary genius. Still, as long as I promised not to cry more than once with Elvis and then start dancing with her, she agreed.

Actually, the only time I remember Tammy shedding any tears is when we hit age fourteen. A beautiful blonde, she had finally decided to pluck her thick, dark eyebrows and trusted no one but me to tame them. We browsed *Seventeen* magazine for inspiration, borrowed my mother's best tweezers, and then alternated the extraction of a few hairs with the application of an ice pack.

"You won't make them too thin, will you?" Tammy asked, wincing with each yank as she lay across the foot of my bed.

"Of course not!"

"Do you (ouch!) think anyone will (ouch!) notice?" A few fat tears leaked from the outer corners of her eyes and trickled down, into her ears.

"You're going to look great!" I handed her a tissue. "Just relax and dry your ears."

The next day at school, Tammy surprised everyone (especially me) by showing up not with the shapely, understated, and natural-looking brows I created. Apparently she had continued the pluck fest on her own and now had virtually no eyebrows at all. And she still looked gorgeous!

Then came 1977. Three things made it a bad year for me: Elvis Presley died, Farrah Fawcett left the cast of *Charlie's Angels*, and I disco-danced in public.

Looking back, I should have heeded my self-preservation instinct to stay home and watch *The Waltons*, but *nooo*. Amid the transportation planning, wardrobe critiquing, and flirt rehearsing of several friends in Tammy's living room, I weakened.

"Will you teach me?" I asked.

My friends squealed with the prospect of transforming me from library nerd to dancing queen for our high school's first junior-senior dance of the year. Tammy hurried to her parents' hi-fi set (that's "stereo" for the MP3 crowd, only with poorer sound quality), which was the size of a freezer. She tossed singer Peter Frampton's album aside and replaced it with a recording of KC and the Sunshine Band.

"Okay, Debi," Tammy assured me, "the California Strut is a line dance, and *it's very easy.*"

The only time in history to equal such exaggerated understatement was in 1912 when *The Titanic* was declared unsinkable. Alas, my bootie shaking was a bust. Why? Tammy omitted one teensy, weensy detail — a crucial pivot that she corrected with the group *after* I had left for home.

When everyone else on the gym dance floor that fateful night did an about-face during the song, I continued strutting away with my back to the crowd. Time and again, when I did a 180-degree turn, I alone *faced the entire dancing school body* for about two beats before they all turned their backs on *me*. Finally I slinked away to the darkened bleachers, vowing never to dance in public or in private for the rest of my life.

Unaware of my dance floor disaster, Tammy boogied on — her feathered blonde hair swishing choppily in the strobe light. On her face I saw the familiar wide smile from our playground days, a smile that said, "This is *fun!*" How did that girl always manage to have fun in situations that tied my stomach in knots?

Throughout our teen years, Tammy remained my very best friend even though we differed in many ways:

She succeeded with boys; I excelled with books.

She sparkled in her drill team outfit at the football games; I stumbled in my marching band uniform.

She enjoyed life; I endured it.

Recently, when an infomercial aired promoting a collection of 1970s disco music, I thought of Tammy. Before every school dance, I had agonized about going. She always told me, *"Just have fun!"*

Twenty-some years later, the advice finally took.

I told my eight-year-old to flick the living room light on and off quickly: instant strobe light. I grabbed my thirteen-year-old to stand with me in front of the oldies infomercial and cranked up the volume. Giving her a wide smile, I said, "Let me teach you the California Strut."

This time, I got it right.

* * *

Young women will dance and be happy, . . . I'll convert their weeping into laughter, lavishing comfort, invading their grief with joy.

JEREMIAH 31:13 MSG

the new neighbor

Judy Hampton

· ·

"A good friend is my nearest relations."

THOMAS FULLER (1732)

I heard the sound of air brakes hissing outside my kitchen window. Glancing out, I saw a huge moving van parked across our street.

Great! New neighbors are finally moving into that empty house, I thought.

Before the movers could unlock the huge doors on the back of the truck, our children, Doug and Joani, walked right over to check out the situation.

They returned soon with good news. "Mom, they have kids the same age as Doug and me," Joani said. "I already like them!"

It wasn't long before I met their mom. She was a Swedish beauty with shimmering blonde hair, periwinkle blue eyes, and a welcoming smile. "Hi, there, I'm Judy Hampton," I said, greeting her warmly.

"My name is Judy too!" she exclaimed. In a matter of minutes we discovered we had a lot in common. As the weeks passed, our kids played together endlessly. My new neighbor was either coming to my house to get her two children or I was walking across the street to retrieve mine. We always had time for a brief visit. Judy and I would pick up right where we left off the day before. She loved being a mom, wife, and homemaker, and I soon discovered Judy was the quintessential housekeeper.

In time our conversation turned to spiritual things. I was a fairly new Christian, and I was passionate to share how Christ had changed my life. Judy listened attentively.

"We're a religious family too," Judy replied rather matter-of-factly. But from that point on, our conversations always moved to other issues.

Mondays could always find me doing endless piles of laundry and cleaning my house. I loved getting my household tasks done in one day so I could free up the rest of the week for more important things. On one of those Mondays I stood at my kitchen sink loading the dishwasher. Glancing out the window, I saw Judy place something in the mailbox on my front porch. Quickly running to the front door, I asked enthusiastically, "Hi, there! Do you have a surprise for me?"

"Well, not exactly. My father-in-law died recently and my mother-in-law gave us his car. I was vacuuming the trunk when I came across this religious book. I thought you might like it because you are so religious."

I stood there a bit dazed, trying to visualize someone actually vacuuming out the trunk of a car. I couldn't recall ever doing such a thing.

"Thanks, Judy. That's so thoughtful of you." I noticed the book was *The Late Great Planet Earth* by Hal Lindsey. I didn't have the heart to tell her I'd already read it. After all, I was *so* religious!

Thinking quickly, I looked up at my neighbor and said, "Judy, I just read a book *you* might enjoy. It's about the Christian family, written by a pastor in your denomination. It's practical and so insightful. I've learned so much about what God says about the family. Would you like to read it?"

"Thanks! I love to read," she responded enthusiastically.

I dashed to our bookcase, got the book, and gave it to her. I waved good-bye and resumed my endless list of chores. About two hours later there was a knock at my door. I was a bit miffed at the interruption to my routine. I opened the door and there stood Judy, tears streaming down her face.

"Oh my goodness, what's the matter?" I gasped.

"Judy, nothing's wrong. I just started reading the book and found I couldn't put it down. I read straight through to the very last page. I realized today what was missing in my life — a relationship with Jesus Christ! The author offered a simple prayer to receive him as Savior, and I prayed the prayer right in my living room. Judy, I can't describe how I feel, but I am so excited! I have been laughing and crying at the same time. I knew I had to tell you."

By now tears were streaming down my face too. No wonder they call it the "Good News"!

That day, God made us family. Judy was my new sister-in-Christ.

. . . .

I find myself praying for you with a glad heart. . . . There has never been the slightest doubt in my mind that the God who started this great work in you would keep at it and bring it to a flourishing finish on the very day Christ Jesus appears.

PHILIPPIANS 1:4, 6 MSG

falling in love

Penny Williams

. . . .

*God won't give me anything I can't handle;
I just wish he didn't trust me so much.*

MOTHER TERESA

I had been a single parent for eighteen years when someone unexpectedly entered my life. He was compassionate, intelligent, funny, and, best of all, he made me feel like I was the most important person in his world. Though we lived a distance from each other, he would often make the trip after work to meet me for dinner. Evenings passed quickly as we shared the highlights of our day, our love for our families, and had discussions of shared spiritual values and principles that were important to us.

The months passed quickly and our bond grew closer. One evening the phone rang. "Penny, could we attend my church tomorrow and then go to Bahama Breeze for dinner?" Excitedly, I accepted. Tom attended a large dynamic church we enjoyed being a part of, and the restaurant he chose was where we had our first date. During dinner the easy flow of conversation and laughter emphasized how well our relationship was developing and how compatible we were as a couple.

Tom pulled out a travel magazine. "Penny, if you could go anywhere in the world, where would you like to go?"

Puzzled, I looked at him, trying to read what he was thinking. I stammered, "Tom, I don't understand." Taking my hand in his, he held it tenderly while looking deeply into my eyes. My heart pounded as he expressed his love for me and his desire to spend the rest of his life with me. Believing the most amazing dream had just come true, I accepted. The rest of the summer passed quickly as we made plans for the wedding and excitedly looked forward to sharing our lives together.

As fall approached, the time grew closer for me to resume my ministry schedule, which involved weekend travel. As I prepared to leave for the first conference, Tom expressed his reluctance to having me go. I assured him I too was going to miss our time together, but expressed the desire God placed in my heart for ministry. Tom teasingly responded, "I'll be the great-looking guy in baggage claim area, waiting for a pickup." I smiled back at this sweet, gentle man I loved.

The first conference of the fall is always exciting, filled with lots of activity and time to catch up with staff members after the busy summer. This fall, however, I found myself unusually restless. In the quiet of the night, I wrestled over my relationship with Tom. Not wanting to believe God was asking me to give up this relationship, I sought out the counsel of Donna, my close friend and director of the conferences. Together we talked and prayed as I sorted through my relationship with Tom.

After making the return trip home, I walked the long corridor to the baggage claim area. Looking up, I saw Tom waiting. My heart leaped at the sight of him — then sank, knowing what I needed to do. It was late and I chose to keep the conversation light.

The next night when he picked me up for dinner, Tom appeared to be deep in thought. Our usual animated conversation of shared experiences and dreams was reduced to a silent reluctance to talk until Tom said, "Penny, I missed not having you here."

"Tom, I believe God has placed me in ministry."

"Penny, I need you to make a choice. I believe you can't give the time necessary for a good marriage and be in ministry at the same time."

Sadly, I knew my dream with Tom was ending. I responded thoughtfully, knowing my heart first belonged to God. I had been internally wrestling with this issue for several weeks. A decision had to be made. It was hard for me to form the words. "Tom, God has placed me in ministry. I can't marry you."

A painful silence clouded the rest of our dinner and the ride home. Silently, Tom walked me to the door. For the first time since meeting, our words were strained and carefully chosen as we said our good-byes.

I longed for the companionship and security that Tom provided. I loved our dinners together and the lively conversation of our shared interests and future goals. However, I realized I was in a relationship with a man who was not interested in having me pursue my dreams, and he did not support my passion for ministry activities. I had to choose between being God's woman or Tom's wife.

Today, I'm still a single parent, and I'd still like to be married when the right man comes into my life. Until then, I am much happier knowing I sought godly wisdom from the Bible and from Donna. I enjoy the work of my private counseling practice and the opportunity to pour my extra time into ministries that are furthering God's kingdom agenda.

It feels good. It feels right.

. . . .

I will instruct you and teach you in the way you should go;
I will counsel you and watch over you.

PSALM 32:8

come to supper, child

Thelma Wells

· ·

Turn your eyes upon Jesus; look full in his wonderful face.

HELEN H. LEMMEL

"Humble" comes from the word *hummus*, meaning "earth" or "brought down low."

Yes, the Creator of the universe who flung the stars into space is also a very down-to-earth God. Why was Jesus "brought down low" — why did he come down to earth in our form?

I was pondering that thought one day as I was busy in the kitchen, my "hive of five" grandkids buzzing around the living room. I put dinner on the table and gave the "y'all come" signal. My grown children and their children began to make their way toward the feast and the smells of my home-cooked turnip greens, buttered carrots, okra gumbo, mashed potatoes, brisket, baked chicken, and corn bread (with ice cream waiting in the freezer to top it all off a little later)!

But two of my darlin's were too busy playing to answer the call. "Alyssa! Alaya!" I called again. Still they paid no attention. So I did the only thing I could do. I went over to where they were engrossed in their baby dolls and scooted down on my achy ol' knees to look them in the eyes.

Now I had their full attention. "Girls," I said with loving firmness, "did you not hear me calling you?"

They shook their heads no, their dark braids flying, their brown eyes wide with surprise.

"Well, sweet things, now that I have your attention, help your old Grammy up and let's go eat."

Together the girls tugged on my arms and off we went toward the banquet.

As I walked with them, I thought about having to go to all that trouble, to physically scoot down low to get the attention of my granddaughters. It was then I realized that this is exactly what Jesus did for me.

God had a wonderful feast prepared for us in heaven and he called his people to come and eat and enjoy! But most often, caught up in their own little dramas, they ignored his call. So, in the form of his Son, Jesus "scooted down low" and became one of us. Why? To get our attention, to meet us eye to eye — to take us by the hand and lead us to the feast.

Are you distracted by a dozen playthings of this life today? Turn around. He's there, waiting to meet you eye to eye. Supper's on the table and all he wants is the pleasure of your company.

Take his hand, child. Trust him. Then follow the Savior to the feast of God's goodness and enjoy!

. . . .

I will fear no evil, for you are with me; . . .
You prepare a table before me.

PSALM 23:4–5

a kiss from god

Danika Protzman

. . . .

Disappointment, if not given to God, becomes discouragement.
Discouragement leads to depression.

KAY ARTHUR

*L*ast year when hardship hit my dear friend Linda's household, she found herself very discouraged. It all started after September 11, 2001, when her husband, along with many of his colleagues, were laid off from their jobs.

After his layoff, Kirk searched for another position while they emptied their savings account and used all remaining resources to live. After taking a new job with a huge reduction in salary, they decided to sell their home and move to a more affordable house that would be more in line with his new salary. They put their 3,000-square-foot house on the market and waited, and waited, and waited some more. After twelve months, three realtors, and no buyers, their home was repossessed.

During that time, Kirk's new company reorganized and cut 150 employees, including Kirk. While he searched for another job, they moved into a 1,300-square-foot, three-bedroom house, but were only able to stay for a short time. To make ends meet they again had to move into an even smaller home.

Linda felt like life was a downhill journey with no reprieves. Very discouraged, she went to a thrift store looking for hidden treasures. It was more of a distraction than a shopping trip. She loves beautiful china and went first to the housewares area of the resale shop. Her eyes were drawn to a blue and white saucer with gold trim. She recognized the pattern — Royal Albert English bone china — a favorite of hers. But the teacup was missing. Thinking she could use it under a plant, Linda purchased the saucer for under a dollar and brought it home.

About four months later Linda visited another thrift store in a different city and was browsing through the dishes. Her eyes were suddenly drawn to a teacup — not just *any* teacup, but a blue and white teacup from the Royal Albert English bone china collection. This cup was missing its saucer, but it was the perfect match to the saucer she had purchased in the other thrift shop.

Linda's thoughts were jumbled. Was this a coincidence or was it a kiss from God, an encouraging moment in time when he reminded her of his love for her in the middle of a thrift shop?

The financially challenging circumstances her family was experiencing were not resolved quickly, but that day Linda realized God knew her intimately, right down to understanding her love of china. The cup and saucer became a tangible marker in her life — reminding her that in the middle of life's most challenging circumstances, he understands our hurts, longs to comfort us, and wants us to focus on hope and a future.

Today the beautiful blue and white Royal Albert English bone china cup and saucer are displayed on a shelf in her kitchen as a reminder of God's love and compassion. She is teaching me that when the circumstances of life seem overwhelming and overbearing, God still cares. And his desire is to give us hope and a future in the midst of life's most difficult challenges.

. . . .

"For I know the plans I have for you," declares the Lord,
"plans to prosper you and not to harm you,
plans to give you hope and a future."

JEREMIAH 29:11

my eccentric tante liesel

Margaret K. Becker

*Some lives, like evening primroses,
blossom most beautifully in the evening of life.*

CHARLES E. COWMAN

*M*arch blew into Ohio. Snow swirled, drifted, and piled against our garage door, but we were heading south. Florida sunshine and a visit with my favorite aunt beckoned. Tante Liesel (German for Aunt Liesel) had recently entered a nursing home in Louisville, Kentucky.

Approaching the city, my thoughts turned to yesteryear — extended summer vacations, my aunt's untamed rose garden, living and dining room walls covered with Uncle Richard's oil paintings, and the infamous mermaid painted on the sea-green bathtub wall.

I'll never forget the day Tante Liesel summoned my cousin Rich and me for lunch with a toot on Rich's trumpet. Or the sweet strains of Tante Liesel's lute as she sang "My Old Kentucky Home" in her slight German accent.

Being around this dear eccentric whirlwind for short periods of time was delightful — but *living* with her was often a challenge. My uncle's attempts to get a word in edgewise were legendary. He finally had his say after her strokes, and he cared for her faithfully until his health failed. His death and God's provision had brought her here — to the nursing home where we were visiting her.

Fuchsia azaleas splashed their welcome as we entered the grounds. Fresh mown grass scented the air. Mixed emotions surfaced as we climbed the wide sandstone steps. A cheerful foyer greeted us as we walked through sturdy oak doors. I checked the resident directory and found her name: Liesel Paulmann — Room 310.

The elevator stopped near the nurses' station. The head nurse directed us to her room. "Hello, Tante Liesel. It's Margaret and Ray from Cleveland," I announced, reaching for her wizened hand through the raised side rails. My tiny aunt was scrunched down in her bed, a shadow of the robust woman I had known in childhood. A toothless grin spread across her face — that same familiar face that had greeted me years earlier on summer visits.

During the six summers I spent with Tante Liesel, I learned about her journey across the Atlantic Ocean. As a young immigrant who didn't speak English, she faced many challenges. Working hard as a housekeeper for wealthy families, she saved her money for two years until she had enough to send for her sweetheart. I loved the story of how Tante Liesel, with her earnings, paid Uncle Richard's passage to America by boat.

. . . .

"Tante Liesel, I'll tie this pretty balloon to the rail so you can see it better," I said. Her eyes followed the bobbing red sphere. She pointed to it frequently — chuckling and ahh-ing. Her words were garbled, except for a few snatches of actual phrases. Faded blue eyes twinkled in recognition and her extravagant gestures communicated joy. Tante Liesel's irrepressible spirit and effervescence spilled over everyone in the room.

During the years I spent rearing my children, often bogged down with mundane tasks, sometimes frustrated or depressed, I remembered the lilting songs my once robust aunt sang as she hung out laundry on a bright windy day. The recollection of her dramatic rendering of old folk poems lifted my spirit.

When my attitude needed adjustment, I recalled her courage as she weathered life's storms — her artist husband's infidelity, her only son's accidental loss of his right eye, and the trauma of being confined in a state mental hospital after a major breakdown during menopause. That was over forty years ago. Love and forgiveness had been the key to her sanity and to her positive response to life. I tried to capture her enthusiasm, her faith, her resiliency.

These memories prompted me to sing "Jesus Loves Me" to her. She became quiet and then I heard it. "Y-e-s!" — as only she could say it. I prayed the Lord's Prayer. She listened intently until something distracted her. I held her hands and continued to pray. My eyes saw this little woman, but my heart held a reflection of the vibrant woman of yesteryear.

Too soon it was time to leave. I kissed her beneath the thinning topknot and lovingly bade her farewell with the familiar German phrase *"auf wieder sehn"* (till we meet again).

Just as plain and dear as in the past, she answered, *"Auf wieder sehn."*

Tears trickled down my cheeks as I retreated from the room. I stumbled into the washroom, splashed cold water on my face, and left the building.

Three weeks after our visit, Tante Liesel went to her heavenly home.

"Auf wieder sehn, Tante Liesel."

. . . .

I thank my God every time I remember you.

PHILIPPIANS 1:3

a little bit of wonderful

Cathy Gallagher

> A moment's insight is sometimes worth a life's experience.
>
> **OLIVER WENDELL HOLMES SR.**

*A*s my friend Rosie and I climbed to our seats in the steepest, highest section at the Van Andel Arena in Grand Rapids, Michigan, I hoped the evening would bring a little bit of encouragement into my depressing circumstances. But I didn't know that I would experience an insightful moment and discover the answer to the question I had been wrestling with for weeks: *What do I do now?*

I was between jobs again, going through my third unwanted career transition in eighteen months. I felt sad, angry, dejected, and worried that employers would view me as unhirable because of a dismal employment record. Attending the concert with Rosie was a pleasant break from the drudgery of job-hunting, which was not going well. I had lost my last position on the heels of 9/11, and corporate America wasn't doing much hiring.

As we settled into our seats, Rosie and I joked about our bird's-eye view of the stage and main floor far below us. Then the concert began. Memories of delightful moments from my youth filled my mind as Neil Diamond sang the songs that had captured my teenage heart several decades earlier.

Usually at such events I looked out at the stage from a main floor seat. I was intrigued by how different the activity on stage appeared as I looked down from high above rather than from a seat down on the main floor.

The intricate, perfectly timed movements of everyone and everything involved in the concert were fascinating to watch. Musicians took their places at precise moments. Props were placed on the stage and removed in seamless precision. The multicolored lights created a kaleidoscope of patterns as they danced around the arena. Neil Diamond's movements were synchronized to the beat of his music.

Toward the end of the concert, a baby grand piano was raised onto the stage directly below us. Rosie nudged me and whispered, "Oh, Cathy, Neil's going to play!"

From my high-rise view, I watched Neil Diamond slowly approach the piano and lovingly stroke its exquisite wood-grain top. Reverently, he said, "Look at this beautiful piano. Some people see a piano as an inanimate object, but I see it as an explosion of potential because of all the songs yet to be written on it."

It was an insightful moment. I didn't hear another song in that concert. I was too busy thinking about what Neil Diamond's statement had stirred up in me. I remembered the Bible says God created people in his image (Genesis 1:27), and I saw myself as God sees me — as his explosion of potential because of all the untapped skills and talents inside me, waiting to be released and used in a new job, the one I hadn't found yet.

Wow! I thought. *Unemployment is like that piano — filled with limitless potential. What I do between jobs matters. I can choose to keep my potential locked inside of me by worrying, complaining, and bad-mouthing my abilities and circumstances. Or I can choose to release my potential by embracing the opportunities unemployment contains, such as the time to look for a job and the freedom to accept interviews without having to ask for a day off work!*

I realized I didn't only have a bird's-eye view of the concert; we had a "God's eye" glimpse of how differently circumstances look from where he sits, high above us, looking down from heaven.

I had been looking at my joblessness from a ground-floor view, seeing personal and professional failure and limitations. God, however, was looking at my potential and at everything he created me to become. He could see what I couldn't — how my past experiences and present job-hunting efforts connected to my future.

Suddenly I knew what to do. I needed to rise above my limited view and embrace his broader view. I needed to put "a little bit of wonderful" into every day by treating my unplanned job loss as a springboard for unlocking my untapped potential as he opened new doors of opportunity. I needed to get up every day with hope in my heart because every day was an explosion of job-hunting potential, and only God knew which day would be *the* day I landed the right job.

When I left that concert, I didn't know I would spend the next six months reminding myself: *this could be the day I find a job.* I also didn't realize the door that eventually opened would be right where I spent so much time searching — Michigan's unemployment office. I guess God felt I'd spent so much time there, I might as well get paid for it. I also didn't know God would plant the desire in my heart to develop a Bible study for the unemployed that would put hope back into the hearts of others who had endured my kind of discouragement.

Even though my future was uncertain as I left that concert, I felt like a new woman. I was no longer sad, angry, worried, and dejected. I was filled with hope and determination. I had experienced how God's ways of looking at my life are higher and better than anything I had imagined, and that felt *wonderful*.

"My thoughts are completely different from yours," says the Lord. "And my ways are far beyond anything you could imagine. For just as the heavens are higher than the earth, so are my ways higher than your ways and my thoughts higher than your thoughts."

Isaiah 55:8–9 NLT

pass it on

Thelma Wells

· ·

We turn, not older with the years, but newer every day.

EMILY DICKINSON

*A*t sixty-one years of age, I began to realize my years left on earth needed to be used in a way that would multiply what God has given me, in ways that would be lasting, and in hearts that would go on when God called me home. I prayed about it and waited as God, in his own creative ways, continued to affirm how I was to do this. In fact, the third time someone said to me, "Thelma, I believe God wants you to share the wisdom you've gleaned with other women in leadership ministry who will be faithful to pass it on," I cried and cried. I had no choice, even with my busy schedule, but to obey.

So I have taken on a nurturing, loving, and instructing role for sixty-five women in ministry whom I call the Daughters of Zion.

My formal title in this new endeavor is a "Mother of Zion," but these African-American women of various ages from all phases of ministry — no matter how seasoned — call me Mama T. These sharp, strong women have been called by God to be everything from evangelists, teachers, and preachers to pastor's wives and praise dancers. Two of them, I'm privileged to say, are my own grown daughters.

The group began meeting once a month at my home for a ten-month session. We talk about relationships, unity, time management, health, and healing a broken heart, as well as other issues. Never one to do anything halfway, I got so excited about this new ministry I created notebooks, brochures, handouts, and even homework for my girls.

There are many questions, issues, struggles, or women's ministry questions they need to discuss with someone. This is true even if they've been ministering for years. "Who can I trust?" they ask. "Who can I talk to?"

I feel so privileged to be the mentor that these women can trust — a friend with whom they can let down their hair and be real. One of my spiritual daughters, Priscilla Shirer, said, "I believe in the Scripture that says the older women should teach the young women. I believe there are a lot of young women who think they know everything, and that is so far from the truth."

Cathy, another minister in our group, said, "All of us have the public face, but we have real concerns going on in our private lives."

In the time we've been meeting, I am seeing much fruit, and our time together is incredibly rich.

Has it been a balancing act to handle the new ministry and my other responsibilities?

Oh, girl, yes, yes, *yes!*

But do I wish I'd decided *not* to take on this assignment from God?

Oh, no.

I wouldn't trade this experience for anything. The grand-mother in me loves mothering, loving, and caring for these ladies. It is natural for me, giving out of my area of giftedness. And I have learned in my years of walking with the Lord that what God has ordained you to do, he will sustain you to do.

Is there something that God is calling you to do but you are unsure if it is of him? Be open, ask, pray. I typically ask my Father to confirm what he wants me to do at least three times so I know I am hearing him clearly, especially if the opportunity is going to require a long time commitment. But when he does affirm and you are sure in your heart that you are hearing his voice, relax and begin to follow him one step at a time.

You may make some mistakes and have some challenges as you follow God. Expect that as part of the process. But I can assure you the pain you may feel as you step out in faith and follow his leading is nothing like the pain of regret, looking back and wondering, *What if . . . what if I had listened and obeyed? What might I have been? What might I have done?*

Listen to God's voice to your heart, my friend, as he nudges you toward your place of greatest service and impact.

Then follow with no looking back, no regrets. Finally, watch him fill you up so that you can splash over to bless his children. There is no greater joy.

. . . .

Those who refresh others will themselves be refreshed.

PROVERBS 11:25 NLT

the crooked tooth

Shari Minke

....

The great beautifier is a contented heart and a happy outlook.

GAYELORD HAUSER

I can fix that crooked tooth for you," the dentist said to me.

Humph! I wanted to punch him in the nose! Never having met the man before, since this was the first time I had ever been to his office, I was offended that he didn't introduce himself before offering his comment. He didn't say, "Hello, how are you?" He simply pointed out my lack of perfection!

I surprised my normally shy self by bristling back, "Or . . . we'll just leave it alone."

The insensitive man proceeded to pick up my left hand and, upon seeing my wedding ring, retorted, "Okay, I see you already have your man."

I was crushed! I wanted to scream at him, *No, I don't!* My husband had left me a few months earlier. I wore the ring in hopes of his return.

The dentist's words haunted me. I interpreted them to mean, "Lady, with a crooked tooth like that, you were lucky to get *any* man!" I sobbed all the way home.

Years went by and God brought another man into my life, and he wasn't deterred from marrying me due to my crooked tooth. God used this gentle man to love me and nurture gifts that were hidden within me.

· ·

Time passed. I was teaching an adult Bible class at my church and one of the men in the class was an orthodontist. He approached me after church one Sunday and spoke verbatim the words I had heard fifteen years earlier: "I can fix that crooked tooth for you." This kind soul had no way of knowing what a trigger those words were to my psyche. I disguised my reminder of an old hurt by chuckling and changing the subject.

A couple weeks later, I heard the words from the orthodontist *again*: "I can fix that crooked tooth for you." While riding home, I had a bad attitude. I spouted off to my husband, "If he wants to fix my crooked tooth, then *he* can pay for it!"

The following Sunday the orthodontist approached me and said, "I can fix that crooked tooth for you and it won't cost you a red cent." Guilt washed over me for my previous unkind thoughts as I realized the sincerity of his offer.

I responded, "Wow! That is very generous. Let me think about it."

On the ride home, my husband's response to the offer was, "You can get your tooth straightened if you want, but as far as I'm concerned, your teeth are fine."

I decided to take a survey of those closest to me. I was intrigued by the responses.

My teenage sons informed me, "I never noticed you had a crooked tooth."

My oldest daughter said, "I have crooked teeth. Will he fix mine for free?"

My youngest daughter responded vehemently, "No! You can't get your tooth fixed. That's what makes you Mommy. That's your 'Mommy' tooth." When she was younger, she named one of my teeth the "Queen tooth." It took me a little while to figure out she was referring to the gold *crown* on my back molar! She couldn't remember what it was called, but she knew it had something to do with royalty.

My parents liked my crooked tooth.

My prayer partner Cindy said, "I don't think I would like it if you got it fixed. It would make you look different. It just wouldn't be *you*."

My buddy Jan responded, "You travel around doing comedy characters. They are all imperfect people. I can't imagine any of your 'characters' having straight teeth."

The clincher came when my friend Vickie offered this challenge, "None of us is perfect. If you got your tooth fixed, what would you want to fix next?"

The next Sunday I gratefully declined the orthodontist's offer. His response surprised me. "Years ago I had a lady working in my office who had a tooth that looked almost identical to yours. I offered to fix her tooth, but she declined too. She stopped working for me and I didn't see her for several years. One day I ran into her and noticed she had gotten her tooth fixed. You know what? I didn't like it! It wasn't *her*." With that, we both laughed.

It's been freeing to know the quality of my life is not wrapped up in my physical appearance. In fact, I've decided to *embrace* my crooked tooth — but I do hope people will tell me when I have broccoli stuck on it!

· ·

God judges persons differently than humans do. Men and women look at the face; God looks into the heart.

1 Samuel 16:7 MSG

cleaning up our act

Lynn D. Morrissey

. . . .

Grace is love that cares and stoops and rescues.

John R. W. Stott

One thing that I especially love about my dear friend Jo is that she's always poised for adventure. Over the years we've explored gourmet cooking, painting, and numerous other projects and passions. Though all our intentions have been good, some have fallen flat. Our closet shelves are depositories for unknitted yarn, unwatched exercise videos, and unread books.

Bur rather than let failure defeat us, we lovingly prod each other to keep trying. The pièce de résistance was our home organization phase. This time we were determined to complete *something*. Analyzing the reason for our past derailments, we realized we had never developed a viable plan for success. With each other's help, we knew we could clean up our act.

One Saturday, despite our being knee deep in obligatory end-of-the-week housework, Jo and I cleverly escaped in the name of a good cause and met early at our favorite bookstore. There we purchased every home-organization, house-cleaning, and time-management book known to womankind. We made a day of it and had a wonderful time. For hours we sat in the bookstore café (over breakfast, lunch, and finally dinner), reading, note-taking, and orchestrating a detailed strategy for deep-cleaning our houses. We were dauntless in laying out a battle plan that would have put General Sherman to shame. We were finally declaring a war on clutter, with a surefire blueprint to win. There was no stopping us!

Over eight hours later, exhausted, I invited Jo to my house to share our game plan with my husband, Michael. Though he is always incredibly patient and understanding, I still didn't relish going home alone, knowing that I'd left the house in complete chaos. True friend that she is, Jo was willing to face the music with me.

When Jo and I opened the front door and walked inside, we were amazed at what we saw. The house was spotless! The carpets were vacuumed, the furniture polished, the clutter cleared. From stem to stern, everything was immaculate, shining, and orderly. My home organization dream had materialized without my even lifting a finger!

"Hey, Jo, this is miraculous! Just *reading* those books worked," I exclaimed, laughing.

Hearing our giggling, Michael appeared with his hands on his hips and a smile spreading across his face. "You know, ladies, at first I was skeptical about your organizational crusade. I thought that *doing* might accomplish more than *talking*. But in the end, I was proven wrong. You two met *long* enough for me to organize the entire house!" Amazingly, Michael even offered to help Jo with a few odd jobs when she was ready to tackle her house.

Jo and I have talked about that incident many times since, realizing that though we extended grace to each other, never criticizing our false starts or even our failures, it was my husband, Michael, who was the real grace-giver. In a gracious gesture of generosity, he cleaned and organized our house — a job I considered was mine to do. I thought I had to develop a perfect plan before I could begin. Instead, though I didn't deserve it, Michael rescued me and did the job I had found impossible to accomplish on my own.

With great gratitude I also realized that I do not have to work hard to "clean up my act" or to perfectly understand the deep theological implications of salvation before receiving God's gift of grace. He loves me just as I am. He loves me so much that he stoops down when I am helpless and rescues me from a life of uncleanness. The ultimate Grace-Giver sent his Son, Jesus, to die for my sins to make me clean and set me free. What I could never finish on my own, God finished for me through the death and resurrection of his Son. There is no more perfect act than that!

. . . .

For it is by grace you have been saved, through faith — and this
not from yourselves, it is the gift of God — not by works,
so that no one can boast.

EPHESIANS 2:8–9

a graceful skid

Vicki Tiede

Life is not a journey to the grave with the intention of arriving safely in a pretty and well-preserved body, but rather to skid in broadside, thoroughly used up, totally worn out, and loudly proclaiming — WOW — what a ride!

AUTHOR UNKNOWN

Laurie loved to hop on her Harley and ride down the road with the wind in her face and her responsibilities at her back. She worked full time and had been a single mom for sixteen years to her two daughters. In the last year she had celebrated a reunion with the twenty-six-year-old son she had placed for adoption as a baby. More recently she had taken a stand against alcohol and its grip on her life. Riding her bike, however, was just for her. Laurie reveled in the opportunity to enjoy God's handiwork from behind the handlebars of her Harley while he whispered to her heart and the wind rushed in her ears.

126

On July 24, 2004, Laurie had just returned from a week-long vacation in the northern part of Minnesota. For the past several summers, she and her girls had enjoyed vacationing at the same cabin. This year her girls had to work, so she made the trip alone on her motorcycle. Lounging by the lake with her Bible, journal, and a pile of books had been treasured time. She relished the hours spent alone with Jesus as he assured her of his faithfulness and abundant grace. With his promises freshly planted in her heart, Laurie returned home to see what new things God was about to reveal.

It was early in the afternoon as Laurie rode down a two-lane street that alternately passed through neighborhoods and businesses on her way to wash her motorcycle. Coming upon an intersection, she was momentarily distracted by the unusual number of cars in the left lane as well as cars parked on the street to her right. Turning her attention back to the road, horror struck her heart. A minivan had stopped to make a turn, and Laurie hadn't seen it in time. Now it was too late, and she was only a few feet from crashing into the back of the van. She braced herself for the impact.

As Laurie lay in the hospital, she assessed the damages. Her left wrist had a compound fracture and, following two surgeries, was pieced together with plates and screws — secured in a neon pink cast. Her right wrist, also broken, sported screws and a clumsy thick plaster cast. As a medical secretary, Laurie's career depended on the use of these hands. Was this a cruel joke God was playing on her? To top it off, her hip, pelvis, and tailbone were broken in six places.

"Time," the doctors told her. "Time and complete bed rest will heal these bones." Laurie faced three months on her back and at least two additional months of rehabilitation in an assisted living facility. Concern for her girls, bills that needed to be paid, and missed work added additional weight to her burden.

Laurie had every reason to wallow in self-pity and depression and to cry out to God with her questions and demands: *Haven't I been through enough? I've done so much and I'm tired now. I am going to continue to follow you, but I really need a break!*

As I stood next to Laurie's hospital bed, I shook my head and words escaped me. Laurie accurately interpreted my sense of helplessness. Then her mouth tipped up at the corners and she said, "Hey, guess what! I know that following Jesus doesn't come with the guarantee of a spotless driving record, which ends when I ride my Harley into heaven. I just thank God for graciously sparing my life. Because he protected my unhelmeted head, I've been given another chance to enjoy this life journey. I didn't do a thing to earn or deserve that!"

Laurie knew that while her bike was totaled, her life was not. Laying my hand on her cheek, one of the few places that didn't hurt, I smiled back and said, "Friend, God's love for you is simply more unimaginable than your circumstances."

Laurie's main concern was not the devastation of her current state of affairs. With God's grace, she was determined to enjoy the ride.

. . . .

Trust in the Lord with all your heart and lean not on your own understanding; in all your ways acknowledge him, and he will make your paths straight.

PROVERBS 3:5–6

telling secrets

Deborah P. Brunt

....

Truth is always strong, no matter how weak it looks,
and falsehood is always weak, no matter how strong it looks.

PHILLIPS BROOKS

*W*e sat across the table from each other. I drank a latte. She picked around the edges of an oatmeal-raisin cookie.

We'd met six years earlier, shortly after I moved into the area. In the four years before she and her family moved away, we became great friends. Even after she left, we kept in touch by email.

But now I was just beginning to know her. It was awkward, like a first meeting, only more difficult because — well, because of the secret that had only recently come out.

It was her husband's secret. But seeking to protect — her husband? her family? God? — she'd kept it for a decade, telling almost no one, successfully hiding the truth even from those closest to her. And yet, I'd known her to be bold and strong, willing to expose evil and injustice. I'd known her to be a woman of truth.

In the end, she'd had to run for her life. Her husband, shamed but not repentant, continued on the path he'd pursued so long. His secret out, he alternately tried to deny it, said, "I'm sorry," made threats, and repeated his destructive behavior.

The children, now young adults, were torn and angry — as much with their mom as with their dad. They too had been living with the secret. Only God knows how many facets of their lives that one lie had poisoned. Only God could restore what years of contradiction had destroyed.

With the divorce officially granted, everything my friend had sought to protect lay in shambles. Everything except her relationship with God. "I'm starting over, Deborah," she said. "I don't know what's next, but God is faithful."

She had no job and no good prospects. She hadn't finished college, having quit shortly after marrying. Through all the years afterward, she had not worked outside the home. She'd poured her life into the calling God had given her as a wife and mom.

What's more, she'd continued to be faithful to the man she'd married, the man who had started out following God, but whose behavior increasingly ran counter to God's commands. Now, with the raw truth exposed, so was the incongruity she and the children had helped keep secret, the incongruity between what he appeared to be and who he had become, the lie that ultimately shredded everything he held dear and utterly dishonored the God he claimed to serve.

"I haven't grieved for him at all," she said. "Is that awful? I did grieve for many years, but now I can't." She still said almost nothing about the things she'd suffered.

Sitting, listening to her talk, struggling to know what was appropriate to ask, what was helpful to say, I watched various emotions cross her face — tension, relief, fear, trust, sadness. Astonishingly, I didn't see anger or bitterness.

As she talked about hurt and hope, I suddenly realized how many wives I knew who had lived with similar secrets. Perhaps the husband was an alcoholic, a womanizer, a homosexual, addicted to pornography, or abusive. In each case, he had pretended to be in a right relationship with God while continuing destructive patterns that trashed God's name. In each case, a Christian wife had found herself in a moral dilemma: does faithfulness to a spouse demand silence?

In each case, the wife had helped guard her husband's secret until a crisis brought everything crashing down. I wondered how many other wives at my workplace, in my neighborhood, in our church were still keeping similar secrets, mistakenly believing that, if hidden, the lie would go away.

We rose to leave. I threw away my empty latte cup. She threw away most of her cookie. We hugged and the friend I'd thought I knew drove off into the night.

Crying and praying for my friend, I drove off too. In my mind, these words to Christians from Ephesians 5:8–11 kept replaying: "Live as children of light (for the fruit of the light consists in all goodness, righteousness and truth) and find out what pleases the Lord. Have nothing to do with the fruitless deeds of darkness, but rather expose them."

Surely, exposing the secret wrongdoing of a spouse will involve pain and loss. Surely, the speaking out of the truth must be done in the right way at the right time to the right people. Surely, the courage and grace for such a step can come from God alone.

But suppressing the truth only allows the poison to spread. Suppressing the truth multiplies the pain and loss. Confessing the truth begins the healing process.

My friend has a long road ahead of her, but she'll make it. She will smile and laugh again. No longer bound by the secret, she can now truly live in the light.

* *

Have nothing to do with the fruitless deeds of darkness, but rather expose them.

EPHESIANS 5:11

the coat of many streaks

Pauline Afman

. . . .

It is one of the blessings of old friends that you can afford
to be stupid with them.

RALPH WALDO EMERSON

*M*oney has never been overly abundant at our
house. Over the years, my husband has been
a pastor in small churches. Although his pay-
check seemed stretched to the max, we always made it to the
next week and never went hungry. Since we had six children,
hand-me-downs were welcomed.

A friend knew I needed a winter coat. One day she invited
me over to let me know she had just the coat for me. It had
belonged to her mother who had passed away fifteen years earlier. Holding the coat tenderly, she spoke softly, "I just couldn't
bring myself to part with it before, but I know *you* will appreci-
ate it. Mother only wore it a couple of times."

The coat looked somewhat promising upon first glance, but
when I tried it on, I discovered a few problems. After so many

years in the closet, its age was showing. The lining, which at one time must have been blue, now displayed faded purple streaks. It was tight across the chest and the sleeves were too short, but she thought it looked fine and was so pleased I would be wearing it. I knew if I rejected the coat, I would somehow devalue the love and generosity with which it was given.

I thanked her sincerely and took the coat home. However, I never felt comfortable in it and dreaded each time I had to wear it. My feelings were conflicted because I had always taught my children to be thankful to the Lord for any boxes of used clothing that came our way.

Being in the ministry, I tried not to complain about things I didn't like and couldn't change. My close friend Karen was the only one I ever confided in because I knew she would not repeat a word. So I unloaded my true feelings, and she listened. I knew she understood.

Fall arrived and it was getting chilly, but I procrastinated when it came to getting out the coat. When it got so cold I *had* to wear a coat, I went to the closet and it wasn't there! I looked through all the closets in the house and decided I must have left it at church. It wasn't there either. I told Karen and she again sympathized with me, but said, "Don't worry about it. I'm going to take you shopping for a new coat."

Karen purchased a beautiful winter coat for me that year — one that really fit. It was a gift of love from a friend who cared. I occasionally thought about the missing coat, but was relieved

I didn't have to wear it anymore. Since I had worn the original hand-me-down for one season, it must have appeased the friend who originally gave it to me. She never mentioned it again.

A few years passed, and my husband accepted a call from another church. I was torn; I knew it was what God wanted, but the thought of leaving my dear friend was difficult. Karen and another friend took me out for a special good-bye dinner at one of our favorite restaurants. The meal was delicious, but what came next was even better.

With a twinkle in her eye Karen said, "Pauline, we have a special gift for you. We want you to know how much we love you."

The gift was wrapped in a *huge* box, and I couldn't imagine what it could be. I was a little embarrassed at how much attention we were drawing. I carefully unwrapped the box, lifted the lid, pulled back the tissue paper, and then . . . *I screamed!* Restaurant patrons from every side turned to stare, but I was oblivious to the scene we were creating. You see, in the box lay the missing coat!

With much laughter Karen explained, "I took it, *knowing* I was going to buy you a new one, but I had a problem. I couldn't figure out what to do with it. I threw it in the garbage once, and then felt so guilty I retrieved it." We laughed until we cried.

As we left the restaurant, I told her, "Karen, I am *not* taking that coat home. You will have to dispose of it yourself."

Imagine my surprise when a few months after our move to a new city a letter from Karen arrived and a crisp five-dollar bill fell out. Her note said, "Pauline, this belongs to you. Someone actually *bought* the coat at my garage sale!"

There has never been a time when God hasn't come through when our family had a need. When it came to the coat, it wasn't so much a *need* as a *want*. God knew my heart and used my dear friend Karen to bless me.

....

A friend loves at all times.

PROVERBS 17:17

the wilderness experience

Bonnie Afman Emmorey

. . . .

Honor isn't about making the right choices.
It's about dealing with the consequences.

MIDORI KOTO

*W*hen Chris and her family moved away, I grieved. Our oldest sons were the same age, our husbands were close friends, and we had a very special friendship. Now she was a four-hour drive away, and I missed her greatly. We had no choice in the matter. Her husband's job was the determining factor. Phone calls kept us connected, but it wasn't the same.

The first summer after their move, Chris came up with a great idea—we would *vacation* together! She did the research and found a great house for us to rent on Lake Michigan. It was near Sleeping Bear Dunes, a favorite place of both of our families, so it seemed like an ideal plan. There was enough room in the house for both families, and we could enjoy quality time together.

We shared walks along the beach, roasting marshmallows over bonfires, swimming in the crystal clear lake, and playing pinochle late into the night. A few days into our vacation, we decided to do a day trip to one of our favorite sand dunes.

Standing at the base of the dune is an experience in itself—climbing it is another! With much laughter, we dragged and encouraged each other until we made it to the top. Once there, we decided to walk the three-mile trek up and down several more dunes to the Lake Michigan shoreline.

My sons Nathan and Jordan, eleven and nine years old, and Chris's son Luke, also eleven, were off and running. Our athletic husbands were having a hard time walking as slowly as we were, and before long it was just Chris, Neil (Chris and Arny's four-year-old son), and me.

We passed other hikers making their way back to the starting point, and they assured us the hike was worth the trip. However, I could see the surprise in their eyes when they caught sight of Neil. I knew they were thinking we were total *idiots* to be attempting such a feat with a young child. Chris and I took turns carrying Neil, and then we each took one of his hands, alternately swinging him between us and encouraging him to keep walking. Our enjoyment of the day was only slightly dampened by the hot sun and our growing thirst. We were still busy catching up on months of being separated.

When we finally finished the three-mile hike and reached the shoreline, we were *exhausted*. We waded into the water and refreshed our hot, sweaty bodies. Before long, we were lying on the sand trying to gain strength for the return hike up and down the dunes to get back to our point of origin.

My brain was busy trying to figure out a shortcut back to the cars. I could *not* see us making the trek back the same way we came. It didn't take long to come up with a plan. I quickly shared it with Chris before I broached it with our husbands. "Why don't we send Ron and Arny back the way we came to get the cars, and we'll just walk along this lovely shore until we reach a spot that has car access?"

It made perfect sense to me, and Chris quickly agreed. When we shared the idea with the guys, we could see their concern, but they also knew what we had gone through already, and they hesitantly agreed with our plan. Nathan, Jordan, and Luke thought it sounded like fun and decided to stick with us rather than walking back with their dads.

Now we had a choice — north or south? It was a toss-up. None of us knew what either choice would bring, so we decided to walk south. Ron and Arny embarked on their walk to get the cars, and we began our adventure.

For the first hour of walking, Chris and I stayed together, enjoying conversation and the beauty around us. But before long, the three older boys took off and were outdistancing us significantly. Since the shoreline wove in and out with coves, I tried to keep the energetic boys in sight, but it meant leaving Chris and the lagging Neil behind. On our right was majestic

Lake Michigan, and on our left tall cliffs. There was no choice but to keep walking.

We were completely unprepared for this experience. The sun was beating down and we had not brought sunscreen. We had no food or water and resorted to drinking from the lake when our thirst became too intense. Our small band of survivors stretched out with Nathan leading the pack, followed by Luke and Jordan. The distance between each child was growing.

It was during the second hour of walking that we passed the *monster dune* that went straight up 450 feet. People at the top yelled down to us with barely audible voices, incredulous that we were walking along the inaccessible shore. We kept walking.

At one point, I waited for Chris and Neil to catch up, thinking I could offer a word of encouragement. Chris looked at me with resignation and despair and said, "I know what Hagar and Ishmael felt like when they were sent into the wilderness to fend for themselves. Do you think we're going to make it?"

I didn't have an answer.

It took *seven* miles of walking along the shore before we came to the first opportunity to go inland. Our worried husbands had been unsuccessful at finding anything closer, and when they finally saw Nathan, Jordan, and Luke straggling along the shoreline, they rejoiced and ran out to meet them. Chris and I were still a couple of coves away from our final destination when we saw Nathan racing back with renewed energy to tell us we were almost there! Our wilderness experience was almost at an end.

When we finally met our husbands, we had walked a total of ten miles. The right sides of our bodies were scorched from the sun and our feet were blistered from the sand. The children — including four-year-old Neil — required no recovery time at all. For them it was a fun adventure. However, Chris and I were exhausted, but thrilled to be alive!

It wasn't until later in the week that we were actually able to laugh about what happened. When we checked a map, we discovered if we had turned north instead of south, we would have needed to walk only one mile to reach a spot where we could be picked up by a car. Oh, how we wished we had obtained a map ahead of time and made the *right* choice!

Chris and I decided our wilderness walk had spiritual application far beyond our vacation experience. As Christian women our map is God's Word, which needs to be consulted before important decisions are made. Not only was it a lesson *we* learned, it became a talking point for an important family discussion.

. . . .

Show me your ways, O Lord, teach me your paths.

PSALM 25:4

god listens . . . carefully

Ginger Garrett

. . . .

Rich, fatty foods are like destiny: they, too, shape our ends.

AUTHOR UNKNOWN

I was scheduled to speak to a group of women I greatly admired and adored, the mothers of preschoolers at our church. I wanted to tell them about all of God's wonderful miracles in my life. But I also wanted them to know I was just one of them, a mother who struggles and has very human foibles.

So I prayed earnestly, "Dear Lord, I'm going to tell these women about all the wonderful things you've done for me. But I want them to know how human I am. I want them to see all my faults so that they will know you are the only source of my blessings. So please allow me to be really transparent with these women, and let them see my faults. Oh, yes, and Lord, one more thing: I don't have any time to go shopping before the event, and I need an outfit. Will you please send a clothing catalog in the mail right away? I'll buy an outfit and have it overnighted. Thank you, Lord. Amen."

While I was on my knees praying, I heard the mailman deliver my mail. I went outside, and — praise God! — I immediately felt the weight of a catalog among the stacks of bills. And there it was, the answer to my prayers, to let me know he was indeed listening very carefully: a Frederick's of Hollywood catalog — offering hundreds of different kinds of women's lingerie. And on almost every page, there was an outfit that would let me be transparent, and everyone would see my faults.

My husband is very excited about my prayer life now, but next time, would someone please remind me to pray about my thighs?

* * *

Before they call I will answer;
while they are still speaking I will hear.

ISAIAH 65:24

like a mighty wind

Thelma Wells

· ·

Several years ago I added something to my personal motto:
In Christ you can be the best of who you can be.
I use an acronym "BEES."
Be aware of who you are.
Eliminate the negatives.
Expect the best from yourself and everyone else and you'll be —
Successful."

THELMA WELLS

J try to move through life, taking God at his word, to praise him in all circumstances and to be stable in the storm — even storms with tornadoes.

In 1998, my assistant, Pat Mays, and I were in downtown Nashville, getting ready for a long evening's nap on the twenty-fifth floor of the Renaissance Hotel. Suddenly we heard what sounded like a locomotive trying to make its way into our room. It didn't take long to realize it was a tornado.

Remembering all those tornado safety drills from my school days in Texas, I knew that the bathroom is typically the most stable place to go for protection. With little time to think, I ran to the bathroom and huddled under the sink. To our horror, the building started swaying, sirens blared, and a frantic voice came over the intercom. "This is not a drill! We are having a tornado! Get to the ballroom now! Do not use the elevator!"

"We have to get out of here, Thelma," Pat said. "Now."

I didn't argue.

By the time Pat and I got to the eleventh floor, however, I could barely breathe from the exertion. "I'm not going another floor," I said. "I'm going to die right here. You go on."

Pat had a "don't argue with me now" look to her eyes that said, "I'm not leaving you and you have no choice. Let's go."

After resting, I made it to the fifth floor. A couple of men, spying my obvious predicament, offered to carry me.

"You want to carry me?" I asked and could not help but laugh. "Have you had children yet? You go on, so you can have your children. I'll get on by."

I finally made it, but I was the last one to arrive in the ballroom, and when I stumbled in, I headed straight for a chair and collapsed.

I finally caught my breath enough to look around me. Everyone was either on cell phones or trying to calm down. "I need a drink," said one guest. "I need a smoke," another said.

I soon joined in the chorus with "I need my Bible," and yes, I had carried it with me on my journey down the stairs.

With no Scripture in mind, I opened my Bible to the fourth chapter of Mark — Jesus calming the storm on the Sea of Galilee. When I finished reading it aloud, I began to pray.

We later learned that a second funnel cloud headed for Nashville changed direction.

In Franklin, Tennessee, my fellow Women of Faith speaker Sheila Walsh heard on CNN that "people were praying in the Renaissance Hotel with their hands up." The next time I saw her, Sheila hugged me. Shaking her head she said, in that lovely Scottish lilt of hers, "Thelma Wells, I knew it was you."

Counselors often say that circumstances and other people serve as "bumps" in our lives, bumping into the cup of our lives. Who we really are on the inside spills out in such moments. I can't always say that what spills out of me, when I am bumped, is what I would want Jesus to see. However, this night I was enormously pleased that when faced with a true crisis, and one tornado-of-a-bump, what spilled out of me was faith and trust. Because that happened, others were calmed and encouraged, and Christ was glorified.

Fill up your cup with the Word of God today, and as you are bumped, what spills out will be life-giving to all around you.

. . . .

I pray . . . that you may be filled to the measure of all the fullness of God. Now to him who is able to do immeasurably more than all we ask or imagine, according to his power that is at work within us, to him be glory.

EPHESIANS 3:17, 19 – 21

yellow ribbons

Anne Denmark

. . . .

*Friendship without self-interest is one of the rare and beautiful
things in life.*

JAMES FRANCIS BYRNES

hat were those patches of yellow on our
trees? We could see them from a distance
as my husband, Don, and I drove down
the street toward our home. As we got closer, we realized the
whole yard was dotted yellow! As we pulled into the driveway,
all four hundred large yellow bows came into view. They decorated the cedars, the hedges, and the trellises on the porch. A
huge banner with the words "Welcome Home" hung from the
balcony.

Don had just returned from a three-and-a-half-month mission at a refugee camp in famine-ravaged Ethiopia. His volun-
teer team brought medical aid to the orphaned, the sick, and
the starving. Not having any medical training, I remained at
home managing his medical practice, my business (a gift and

book shop), and taking care of our three young children, ages eight, four, and two.

As our hearts rejoiced at this surprise greeting, I wondered who could be responsible for this extravagant outburst of joy. It didn't take long to discover it was my dear friend Barb. As the brainchild of the whole production, she went to the police department to find out where she could obtain the thick yellow tape used to rope off designated areas. She acquired four large spools and headed to a local flower shop. There she shared her idea with the florist, Darcy, who immediately wanted to participate in the surprise. Barb explained to her, "I have this much money. Please make as many bows as you can." Four hundred beautiful bows later the spools were empty and Darcy's wrists were numb, but the task was completed. Then Barb recruited additional friends to work like busy bees helping to pollinate our front yard with fat yellow bows.

I later asked Barb whatever possessed her to do such a thing and she said, "I just *had* to do it. Don had been away so long and you had waited many months for his return. When the idea came to me, I just had to do it."

Barb's gift was an unselfish act of love I still cherish. It would have been easier for her to feel twinges of jealousy. I had the large storybook home with the wraparound porches, the strong marriage, and the public respect as a doctor's wife. Barb worked long hours serving at the local tea shop, always desiring a fulfilling relationship with her husband. Yet her heart rejoiced with mine over my husband's return. And not just a quiet rejoicing — but with an extravagant outpouring of time and effort.

· ·

Several years later, as Barb and I talked over coffee, I first shared the difficult news of our family's coming move to Oklahoma. Slowly a painful, blank stare filled her face as I searched for a way to soften the reality of the soon-to-come good-byes. Then silence hushed our hearts and misty eyes betrayed our deep understanding. We both knew that our friendship would always remain, but we also knew it could never be quite the same. Distance and the passing of years would reshape our friendship.

Moving day arrived quickly. As we prepared to leave our hometown, many friends, including Barb and her husband, came to see us off. With this gathering of precious folks, we held hands in a huge circle and thanked God for friends and memories.

Three days later we pulled into a new, unfamiliar neighborhood, and there they were — the same yellow ribbons! This time they were hanging from oak trees and from the rafters above the entrance. The front door sported a sign that read, "Welcome Home!"

You guessed it! My buddy Barb had saved those bows all those years and shipped as many boxes of yellow ribbons as she could afford to our real estate agent in Oklahoma. When I called Barb to thank her for the yellow ribbon greeting, she said, "I know this move is so right for you and I just wanted to welcome you home *again*."

What joy it was to my homesick heart to know friendship can travel the distance. Barb is a friend who only wants what's best for me. And the distance between her heart and mine is not really a long distance when measured in love.

. . . .

When others are happy, be happy with them.
If they are sad, share their sorrow.

ROMANS 12:15 NLT

searching for truth

Cathy Gallagher

The Lord is ever calling our wandering thoughts and affections back to himself.

JOHN PHILLIPS

Oh, please, be home, I thought as I lifted the telephone's receiver and dialed her number. I was eager to tell my friend about the book I had just read.

As the phone rang, memories of countless other phone calls I had made over the years to Carol Kent flooded my mind. I met Carol and her husband, Gene, twenty-one years earlier, and we had become good friends. The pattern of those phone calls was always the same:

I would blurt out, "Carol, you'll never guess what I've discovered."

Carol would say, "Tell me."

After I described the advice I discovered in the New Age book I had recently read, she would say, "Cathy, you are *such* a *seeker*."

I thought she was complimenting me. I wasn't ready to see what Carol knew and had tried to help me understand many times throughout the years — I was seeking lasting answers from temporary sources.

Throughout the years I read piles of New Age books and listened to stacks of New Age audiotapes and CDs. I also sought guidance from my weekly horoscope, assurance from fortune-tellers, direction from my astrological chart, wisdom from tarot cards and numerologists, knowledge from psychics, and peace from Eastern Indian spiritual practices. The advice these sources offered never worked for long.

I was brought back to the present moment when Carol answered the phone. Our conversation began as usual: "Carol, you'll never guess what I've discovered."

"Tell me," she said hopefully.

"Do you remember my New Year's resolution to become fit by my fiftieth birthday by exercising and dieting because I thought life would be good if I looked good?" I asked.

She did.

"I went to the mall to buy an exercise outfit and a book to read on the gym's treadmill, noticed a Christian bookstore next to the sporting goods store, and decided to check it out. Seeing all the Bibles in different versions, colors, sizes, and price ranges overwhelmed me. I was about to bolt out the door when I thought: *The greatest book ever written is the Bible*.

"At the same time, one Bible caught my eye. I pulled it off the shelf, opened it, and read a verse and the note telling me how the verse applied to me. Then I bought it."

"Cathy, you bought a *Bible*? Did you *read* it?" Carol asked.

"Of course I did — cover to cover. Then I remembered that when I was sixteen I had asked Jesus into my heart to be the Lord and leader of my life. I was embarrassed that I'd relied on those New Age things all those years, so I prayed, asked God's forgiveness, and recommitted my life to Jesus."

"Oh, Cathy, Gene and I have been praying for twenty-one years that you would find Jesus! I was beginning to wonder if you ever would," Carol admitted.

Then she asked, "What did you do with all of your New Age books and tapes?"

"I threw it all away — four boxes' worth! I still can't believe how much money and time I wasted on that stuff."

Before saying good-bye, Carol and I praised God for changing my physical fitness goal into a spiritual fitness goal, thanked God for answering her prayer of twenty-one years, and rejoiced that, at almost fifty, I had sought and found Jesus, the only true source of lasting answers and advice.

Create in me a clean heart, O God. Renew a right spirit within me. Restore to me again the joy of your salvation, and make me willing to obey you.

PSALM 51:10, 12 NLT

new beginnings

Margaret K. Becker

. . . .

Retirement can be a catastrophe or a commencement, a rocking chair or a launching pad.

LLOYD CORY, *QUOTABLE QUOTES*

he *Sword of Damocles* hanging over my head was about to fall — my husband's early retirement date was set for May 1. Only five months until the big party. I sat at my desk agonizing over the projected changes in my life.

As I wrote in my journal, the words *I'm afraid* flashed red. I recognized a root problem in myself — the fear of change. I continued to write: "I like my life as it is, my rut. What will happen to my social life, my ministry, my quiet time?" My thoughts were all about *me* and how my husband's retirement would negatively impact my life.

I recalled the promise God made to me months before when talk of retirement surfaced. *I will take care of your retirement.*

My retirement? I'm not retiring! Ray is.

Oh, yes, you are — you and Ray are one in me. God's voice was as plain as if he were sitting across from me at the kitchen table.

By New Year's Day I was in turmoil and despair. TV football games blared nonstop. Lunch was over and soon it would be time to start dinner. I wondered, *Is this what I have to look forward to?*

The sixty-degree temperature lured me outside. I tried to disperse my frustration by yanking forgotten fall weeds from flowerbeds. Sniffling, my vision blurring, I carried on the pity party. *I can't do this Lord.*

God spoke to my heart. *Margaret, change your attitude!*
I'll try, Lord, but I need your help.

. . . .

God answered my prayer by revealing my selfishness. What about Ray's plans for the future and God's plans for Ray's life? I needed to understand who was in control! I wanted to say, *Whatever you have for me, Lord, I will receive with joy.* But it was a challenge. My spirit was willing, but my flesh was weak.

For the next thirty days messages came loud and clear. God spoke to me through his word, *Trust in me; lean not on your own understanding.* Then I read a book conveying how God uses retirement as a time of reflection and change. Several magazine articles stressed that much personal and spiritual growth begins through change. Slowly, my attitude transformed to the point of looking forward to *our* retirement.

The first year was the most difficult — learning to adjust to twenty-four-hour togetherness. Some activities remained constant — my Monday morning prayer and accountability meetings and Wednesday night church services. Other activities received modification — frequent luncheon dates with friends, spontaneous shopping sprees, and extra-long telephone conversations.

Creative writing became a new outlet for me. The joy of seeing my byline in print was exciting.

Ray's venture into stained glass art and creative woodwork developed into a small family business. Together we shopped for supplies, selected patterns and color combinations, and entered arts and craft fairs. We were a team — master craftsman and super saleslady!

By faith Abram left Haran, making the journey to the unknown land of Canaan. By faith I journeyed into the unknown land of retirement. God fulfilled the promises he made to both of us. Abram became Abraham, the father of many nations, and I became a retiree content with God's plans and the author of many words written for him.

Change and growth are part of God's plan for us and for all of creation. To fight change is to fight God. To embrace change exemplifies our trust in the Lord. He makes a way where there doesn't seem to be a way.

* *

Why are you down in the dumps, dear soul? Why are you crying the blues? Fix my eyes on God — soon I'll be praising again. He puts a smile on my face. He's my God.

PSALM 42:11 MSG

bubble gum kiss

Karen Coy

. . . .

God diligently trails after us without hurrying us. He speaks to us,
letting us know that apart from him we will never be complete. He
does not just say, "I love you." He constantly shows us how much.

JAN JOHNSON

I sat in the hot tub with tears streaming down my face.
Blindly staring out the huge windows of my Colorado hotel, I hardly noticed the majestic mountain
view. I desperately hoped anyone who walked by the glass
enclosure would simply assume the chlorinated water had
splashed my face. I had never felt more forsaken.

A year earlier, a relationship I had expected to end in marriage had simply ended. I spent the year trying to recover from
the blow of having the path I thought my life would take crumble before me. For a year I sat back and watched as, one by one,
my friends set wedding dates. I hoped my pain wasn't evident
as they excitedly shared their plans. Daily I mentally replayed
angry tapes about grievances that happened during our relationship. A year of unforgiveness. A year of unspeakable hurt.

I was still reeling from the news I'd received right before I left on this business trip to Colorado. I had found out my former boyfriend was getting married and, quite frankly, I was angry. I was the one who was supposed to go off and live happily ever after — not him. It wasn't fair! To make matters worse, every area of my life seemed rocky. I was having financial problems and my career path seemed uncertain. I felt like I was careening down the highway of life, and God had most definitely fallen asleep at the wheel.

Despite my bleak outlook, I didn't want to ruin the weekend I had tacked on to my trip. In an attempt to salvage the day, I forced myself to go to the resort town of Breckenridge and arrived in the middle of their Memorial Day parade. I felt more alone than ever as I watched the floats go by, filled with giggling children waving at their proud parents. As they happily tossed candy to the spectators, the kids lining the street scrambled after the bubble gum and sweets.

Suddenly I realized how badly I wanted one of those pieces of bubble gum. But since it would apparently involve getting down on my hands and knees and knocking children aside, I resisted the impulse. But the desire wouldn't go away. "This is ridiculous," I chided myself. "You are a grown woman. Forget about the stupid gum." Feeling a bit silly at this unprecedented obsession for bubble gum, I finally had to admit defeat as the parade ended and I stood empty-handed.

Slowly I made my way back to my car, which was parked in the lot where the parade floats were returning. My hand was on the door handle when I heard a voice across the parking lot yell, "Hey, lady!" I whipped my head around to see a boy of about twelve waving wildly from one of the floats. I turned to see who the "lady" was, and since no one else was in sight, I realized he was talking to me. "Hey, lady!" he shouted again. "Do you want a piece of bubble gum?"

I stood there absolutely dumbfounded. I slowly nodded my head up and down and managed to squeak out a "Yeah!" In what seemed like slow motion, the boy wound his arm back and lobbed that piece of gum seventy-five feet in my direction. I am no baseball player, but I reached up and plucked that candy out of the air like I was born to catch.

I stared at the piece of bubble gum in my palm as if it were a precious treasure. I smiled, realizing this might simply be the happy ending to one woman's quest for bubble gum. But I knew in my heart it was so much more. I could almost hear God's voice saying, "Karen, I haven't fallen asleep at the wheel. I know and care about your needs — even something as small as a piece of bubble gum. And if I care about your smallest needs, think how much more I care about the big ones."

As I unwrapped the gum and popped it in my mouth, I felt like God was gently reassuring me that he was in control and that in his time, he would provide everything I needed.

That was ten years ago. I'm now happily married to a wonderful man, but I still have that bubble gum wrapper. Each time I come across it, I'm tempted to throw it away. After all, do I really need a piece of crumpled paper to tell me God cares about every hair on my head? But the truth is, sometimes I *do* need this tangible reminder. And so each time I rediscover the treasured wrapper, I smile and think of the day God gave me a "bubble gum kiss."

Therefore I tell you, do not worry about your life, what you will eat or drink; or about your body, what you will wear. Is not life more important than food, and the body more important than clothes? Look at the birds of the air; they do not sow or reap or store away in barns, and yet your heavenly Father feeds them. Are you not much more valuable than they?

MATTHEW 6:25–26

overseas connection

Laurie Winslow Sargent

. . . .

My Christian friends, in bonds of love,
whose hearts in sweetest union join,
Your friendship's like a drawing band,
yet we must take the parting hand.
Your company's sweet, your union dear;
Your words delightful to my ear,
Yet when I see that we must part,
You draw like cords around my heart.

JOHN BLAIN, EIGHTEENTH CENTURY U.S. HYMN WRITER

I was hungry for contact with my American friends. My husband, Gordy, our kids, and I had lived in Haugesund, Norway, for about a year. We'd moved there adventurously when Gordy accepted a job transfer with a Norwegian-owned company he'd worked for in America.

In many ways we loved the country and the friendships we'd made there. Yet I was weary from trying to function all day, every day, in another language. Weary from calculating sock sizes in metric sizes. Tired of deciphering school papers one . . . word . . . at . . . a . . . time, with Norsk-Engelsk dictionary in hand. Embarrassed that my poor Norwegian grammar made my son's friends giggle. And frustrated that I couldn't yet understand the quick-paced foreign chatter on the radio.

How I longed to hear a warm hello from home, in my beloved *English*! I realized how foreigners living in America must miss their own mother tongues.

Even in this age of technology, calling the States was no easy task. The nine-hour time difference — crossing multiple time zones — created a tiny three-hour window when both I and my friends, on opposite sides of the Atlantic, were home *and* awake at the same time. And at a dollar per minute, a breezy twenty-minute chat meant twenty bucks less to pay for *kjott* (meat). It was too extravagant of me to call *just* for companionship. Sigh.

One Sunday afternoon, my friend Bette came to mind. Strangely, I felt an overwhelming need to call her. We hadn't spoken since I'd left America, and I felt a stab of guilt. Of course, I'd had adjustments to make: I had my new baby Elisa to care for as well as six-year-old Aimee and eleven-year-old Tyler. And we were still emotionally recovering from a severe accident Gordy had suffered on the job a month or so before, when he'd been hospitalized with burns.

But Bette had been terminally ill when we'd last spoken. Why hadn't I called sooner?

Suddenly I feared I might have already lost the opportunity to ever talk to her again. A warm memory came to mind: Bette enthusiastically saying, "No matter what, we'll see each other again: here, there, or in the air!" I hoped it would still be here. Or there. Yet even if I were to dial and reach only her grieving husband, Joe, I sensed I still must call.

But when? In Norway, 9:30 p.m. would be just after noon in Kennewick, Washington. Might I catch them just after noon, perhaps after returning from their church service?

I realized that I also longed to call my friend Joanne, in Redmond, Washington, but for purely selfish reasons. To gripe a little. Laugh a little. Talk about everything and nothing in particular. But I couldn't justify the expense of placing two calls. We'd been in touch not long before, when Gordy was injured. He was healing well. No, I'd have to choose. Bette and her husband, Joe, were more important than my own need for casual comfort.

I paced impatiently all afternoon and evening. Eventually Gordy and the kids were in bed. I was sleepy too. But when our pendulum clock bonged on the half hour, I picked up the phone and dialed the long string of numbers.

"Hello?" I heard a welcome response. The connection was remarkably clear — as if I'd called next door.

"This is Laurie, calling from Norway!" I said.

Suddenly I heard an explosion of laughter, cries of "No way!" and shouts of "Praise God!" I was put on a speaker phone.

I felt overwhelmed as I heard a chorus of encouraging voices. Joe. Our long-time friend Sylvia, who'd flown in for the weekend from Pennsylvania. And Bette!

Yes, she was still ill. Yet her enthusiasm and faith encouraged *me*. Then suddenly, on the end of the line I also heard . . . *what? who?* Joanne!? And Chuck, her husband? What were *they* doing there, two hours away from home?

They told me with excitement that they were there to spend time with Bette and pray together. And the instant they'd grasped hands — unbelievably, to pray for *our* family and Gordy in particular — the phone had rung. Bette said they nearly hadn't answered it. They usually turned the ringer off entirely when praying.

They then asked me to join them in prayer, via the speakerphone. I closed my eyes. Remarkably, I felt as if I were in the room shoulder to shoulder with them all instead of half a world away as we lifted our concerns and gratitude to God.

How deeply he cares for us and values our friendships! I called to offer comfort to a friend — but my Lord knew *I* needed it too. Before I ever sensed that I *must* call Bette, God had gone before me, prompting Joanne and Chuck to hop in their car and Sylvia to board a plane — all bound for Bette's.

I suspect that God chuckled at my reluctant decision to call only one friend because of the expense. I imagine he must have rubbed his hands in great anticipation the instant I picked up the phone to dial. For *he* knew at that precise moment five

friends — from three different cities — would be together praying for me and my family on the other side of the world. All
along my great God planned to give me *five* blessings for the
price of one.

. . . .

Do not be afraid or discouraged, for the Lord is the one
who goes before you. He will be with you;
he will neither fail you nor forsake you.

DEUTERONOMY 31:8 NLT

bequest of wings

Cynthia Reynolds

....

He ate and drank the precious words,
His spirit grew robust,
He knew no more that he was poor,
Or that his frame was dust.
He danced along the dingy ways
And this bequest of wings
Was but a book. What liberty
A loosened spirit brings!

EMILY DICKINSON

I peeked in my daughter Jessica's bedroom and found her curled up with a book. "What are you reading, sweetie?" She looked up with a knowing smile and said, "*Anne of Green Gables.*" My heart swelled with joy and I found unexpected tears in my eyes.

All of my pregnancies required an unwanted period of mandatory bed rest. When I was pregnant with Jessica, the doctor ordered *complete* bed rest, and I was terrified. Following two miscarriages, I wasn't taking any chances. I lay there tense and fretful, with thoughts swirling in my head: *Is it okay to walk to the bathroom? Should I lie flat, or can I raise my head a little?*

A friend called to cheer me up and pointed out a simple truth, "You are doing all you can. Worrying won't help. In fact, it might do harm." I relaxed a little. My friend said, "Do you have a good supply of children's books?" I thought she was talking about the cloth books and the *Pat the Bunny* book I had acquired in anticipation of our little one's arrival. But before I could answer, she set me straight. "I'm talking about *Anne of Green Gables, Treasures in the Snow, Five Children and It* — children's books."

I had never heard of most of these books, even though I had been an avid reader when I was young. "No," I admitted.

"Well," she said, "send your husband to the library to get these books for a start. Now, do you have a pencil and paper?" I wrote furiously as she gave me the names of titles and authors.

When my husband got home, I greeted him warmly. Then I handed him the list as if it were a prescription and said, "Go. Go now. Please get me these books." I felt an urgency to have these books in my hands, as if reading them would be the best medicine.

And in a way, they were. When he returned home with the books, I plunged into reading, and from that moment on, I never worried about my unstable pregnancy. I was absorbed in another world — immersed in Anne's heartbreaking childhood and tender optimism, captivated by Annette's hard heart and the miraculous way it was softened, and enchanted by the children who found a sand fairy and learned having your wishes granted is not something to take lightly.

God used the creative gifts of others to bless my heart, my mind, and, ultimately, my body and the tiny person clinging tenuously to life inside my womb. He used those stories to captivate my imagination for noble purposes and steer it away from fear. Other books could have done as well, more adult books. However, the simple truths I was reminded of in these well-written classics calmed me, centered me, and filled me with hope and joy.

Now, ten years later, I stood at my daughter's door, watching her read one of the same books that comforted me when she was growing in my womb. "It's my favorite, Mom," she said with a smile.

God's care for us in such rich and meaningful ways was never more evident to me than at that moment.

Many times when a friend in need has asked for advice, I've handed them a book. "Start with this," I say, knowing it will bring God's deep and abiding comfort — perhaps for generations to come.

Whatever is true, whatever is honorable, whatever is right, whatever is pure, whatever is lovely, whatever is of good repute, if there is any excellence and if anything worthy of praise, let your mind dwell on these things.

Philippians 4:8 NASB

six feet tall — and bald!

Eva Marie Everson

. . . .

Laughter is the shortest distance between two people.

VICTOR BORGE

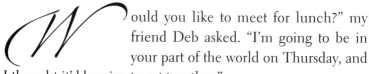ould you like to meet for lunch?" my friend Deb asked. "I'm going to be in your part of the world on Thursday, and I thought it'd be nice to get together."

Although Deb and I live in the same city, there's a forty-five minute distance between us. It seems we're always looking for excuses to "get together."

"I'd love to," I answered.

"But let me warn you, it's too hot to wear a wig. I hope you don't mind being seen with a bald woman."

My valiant friend was successfully battling cancer. Chemo's only visible side effect had been the loss of a full head of hair. "I don't mind," I assured her.

A few days later I sat across the table from Deb in a booth at a local restaurant where we exchanged news about our families, our work, and ourselves. She sat straight and tall as overhead lights cast reflections and halos about her head, completely unfettered from the questioning stares from other patrons. "I'm determined to get through this with grace and humor," Deb told me. "So far . . . so good."

"Excuse me," our waitress said from the side of our table, looking at Deb, "do you mind if I ask if you have cancer? Are you undergoing chemo?"

"Yes, I am," Deb answered.

"Would you mind going to the hair salon a few shops down the mall?"

Our brows shot straight up. *Do what?*

"My friend — the owner — was just diagnosed with cancer . . . and she's just not handling it well."

Deb smiled. "I'd be happy to!"

"I know you don't even know her," the waitress continued.

"I always say there are no strangers in the world, just new friends I've yet to meet," Deb countered. "Don't worry. Leave everything to me."

An hour later I followed along as Deb, nearly six feet tall and completely bald, walked into the salon. "I'm here for a perm," she exclaimed to the gawking faces. Then she laughed. "I'd like to speak to the owner, please."

A petite, dark-haired woman approached. "I'm the owner," she said. "May I help you?"

Deb asked if there was a place they could talk. "Someplace private?"

I could sense the woman was nervous. Why would a bald woman want to talk to the owner of a small hair salon? To buy a wig, perhaps? Hopefully not to complain about a hair product gone bad . . .

"Sure," she said, then escorted us to the back where — amongst stacks of papers and boxes of shampoo and conditioner — a small desk was flanked by a few chairs. "Will this do?" she asked.

Deb and I sat and Deb got right to the point. "Your friend from Gleason's Restaurant asked me to come down and speak with you. I have cancer."

The shop owner, whose name tag read "Maria",* sat down. "I was just diagnosed," she said.

"I know," Deb replied, her voice steady. "I want to talk with you about that."

For the next half hour, Deb shared her story and then answered Maria's questions. Shoulders — straight with tension when we'd first sat down — were now inching downward. In no time Maria was laughing at Deb's anecdotes and sharing some of her own more humorous moments of dealing with the disease they shared. Finally Deb asked, "Can we pray with you?"

Maria nodded. "Please."

We prayed together and were then escorted from the back of the shop, past the boxes of stored product, and down a wide

---

* Name changed.

aisle between sinks and salon chairs. All eyes were on us, questioning: *What was so funny back there?*

Just as we were about to reach the front door, it swung open and a distinguished gentleman walked in. After one look at Deb, he stopped short.

"I'd run the other way if I were you," Deb said, loud enough for everyone to hear. "When I came in, I had long hair. All I asked for was a trim!" She ran her hand over her smooth, shining head.

"*What?*" the man gawked.

"Seriously," Deb answered, never blinking nor missing a beat.

"Hey," Maria called from behind us, laughing, "you'll run off all my customers."

Deb looked over her shoulder and smiled, then cut her eyes back to the man. "I'm just kidding," she said with a chuckle. "I just have cancer."

When we turn our trials over to God, he truly *does* turn our heartache into laughter, even if it means sending a bald woman into a hair-styling salon.

* *

God has brought me laughter, and everyone who hears about this will laugh with me.

GENESIS 21:6

173

the royal coffers

Jeanne Zornes

In the greatest difficulties, in the heaviest trials, in the deepest poverty and necessities, he has never failed me; but because I was enabled by his grace to trust in him, he has always appeared for my help. I delight in speaking well of his name.

GEORGE MUELLER

*M*ail for you," I told my high school daughter as I picked her up after school on that cloudy December day. In half a year she'd graduate, and college decisions weighed heavily on us.

"Probably another 'I'm-sorry-but' letter," she said, wiggling her thumb through the seal of an envelope I'd brought along. The sender was a university where she had applied for a high-stakes scholarship.

I held my breath, afraid to hear the news.

A few months before, we'd entered the parenting era of college bills. Her brother, a year ahead in school, had just started at the junior college three blocks from our home.

Scholarships covered all his tuition there. But he'd have to finish his engineering degree elsewhere. For our daughter's violin studies, she'd need to go somewhere else — but where?

Two in college — on a teacher's pension. It was an impossible equation. Retirement rules had pushed their dad out of his thirty-one-year job. Now he substitute taught for less than half of his former wage. I worked out of our home while providing care for his elderly mother, who'd just beat cancer. Giving to God's work still came first. We shopped garage sales, clipped coupons, and did without. We lived in a small tract home and drove older cars. The kids and I substituted on newspaper delivery routes for "fun money."

Yet while I tried to be content, a corner of my heart resented the constant financial pressure. With greater college expenses ahead, I'd asked the Lord, "How are we going to do it?"

Then for our daughter, one substantial scholarship possibility glittered. Our community always chose a queen for its big spring festival. With the rhinestone crown came a $5,000 scholarship. But the Cinderella dream had a price: two hundred appearances at a grueling pace, including scores of parades out of town. My daughter saw it as jeopardizing her dreams of graduating with a hard-earned 4.0 GPA, serving as golf team captain, and playing her violin concerto in the spring concert.

Though I told her I'd respect her decision, I'd pushed, thinking I was helping God "work it out." She wrestled over taking on more commitments with her life already too full —

despite the scholarship at stake. I noticed her become increasingly moody and uncertain as she prayed — and I prayed. Finally came the day of decision. To compete, she needed to attend a mandatory meeting that afternoon.

What will she decide? What's your will, God? Doubts churned inside me as I waited in the car for her that rainy November afternoon. She came, thrust her bulging backpack and violin in the backseat, then got in beside me, her eyes straight ahead. I saw tears streaking her cheeks as she said, "I just can't do it. It's not me. Let's go home. I have too much homework tonight."

So we went back to apply for general scholarships, hoping some of them would come through and take the bite out of the bill — wherever she attended. Months earlier, her principal had nominated her for a prestigious full ride at a state university. Out of hundreds of top-notch nominees, only twenty-five in the state would be chosen, based on academics and leadership. But she'd never held a student body office. Her possibility of winning seemed as remote as landing on Pluto.

And so, two weeks after the royalty competition cutoff, the official-looking envelope arrived from that university. I debated. Should I leave it on her bed so she'd get the bad news in private? Or should I take it along when I picked her up from school? I took it along.

"Here comes another disappointment," she muttered. She pulled out the letter as I pulled out of my parking space.

"Mom!" she exclaimed. "I got it — *the full ride*! Tuition and housing, worth $14,000 a year, renewable all four years with a 3.5 GPA!"

I suddenly became a distracted driver! I could only say, "Praise God," over and over.

Three months later, our son won generous tuition scholarships to the same university. His housing bills still loomed, but God had spoken through those scholarships. We needed to trust him to provide the rest from the royal coffers of heaven, however he worked that out.

Living simply for the Lord used to be so simple when life wasn't so expensive. But God used the stretch of lean finances to remind me that he excels at financial planning. When he disposed of what I proposed, he had something much better. He supplied our need and he bolstered my faith.

Who needs a rhinestone crown when your Father is heaven's King?

* * *

*We humans keep brainstorming options and plans,
but God's purpose prevails.*

PROVERBS 19:21 MSG

"can anything good happen at 5:30 a.m. in the airport?"

Lucinda Secrest McDowell

....

When God closes a door, he often opens a window.

ANONYMOUS

I couldn't have been more discouraged professionally. As I packed to leave the Christian Booksellers Convention in California, I wept and wailed at God.

"I give up. This writing stuff is way too hard. No one likes my ideas anyway. If I quit now, all my unwritten books won't even be missed!"

My current book project had been circulating through several publishing houses to no avail. And now a literary agent had met with me and said, "No one wants this book, Cindy. No one will publish it, and no one will buy it."

Still, I refused to accept the futility and finality of her statement. I clung to the idea that my book on wisdom shared by women turning fifty was a needed and positive way to encourage my own generation of aging baby boomers.

Through my sobs I went to God in prayer. "Lord, please show me your path for my writing career. I'm willing to give it all up, but I'm also willing to persevere. Which will it be? You are in control and I submit myself to your will. Amen."

It seemed I had barely cried myself to sleep when the alarm rang at five o'clock the next morning for my shuttle to the airport. Upon arrival, I wandered through security to my gate looking, I'm sure, like the failure I felt myself to be.

I sat down in the waiting room with some fiction authors and we began to chat about the convention. Soon another woman joined us and introduced herself as an editor for a Colorado publisher. Our consensus was that we were all eager to get home to our families. As the loudspeaker announced boarding flights, everyone stood up to disperse to various gates.

Turning to the editor, Mary, I said, "Well, now that you're leaving the convention, is there one manuscript you had hoped to acquire but didn't?"

"As a matter of fact, there is," she replied. "My boss really wants a book on baby boomers turning fifty."

My jaw dropped open and, in the few seconds we had before boarding, I briefly explained my book proposal and asked if I could mail it to her.

"You bet!" Mary replied.

My long cross-country flight was filled with new hope — not just the hope that this fifth book might finally find a home but a renewed confidence that God was still guiding my steps and ordering my paths, even as I tentatively approached my own half-century mark.

This year, four million people turned fifty, and I was one of them. What have I learned so far? What truths will continue to guide and sustain me in the rest of life's journey? Well, at least one of them is that God is in control and he will open and close doors at will. All he asks is for us to relinquish our control and step out in faith and obedience.

By the way, my book was published as a direct result of that early-morning airport encounter.

<hr />

I love the Lord, because He has heard my voice and my supplications. Because He has inclined His ear to me, therefore I will call upon Him as long as I live.

PSALM 116:1–2 NKJV

holding god's hand
in the dark

Thelma Wells

*Take the first step in faith. You don't have to see the whole
staircase; just take the first step.*

DR. MARTIN LUTHER KING JR.

*a*s a scared little seven-year-old girl, I would sit in a
narrow, dark, musty closet for hours at a time. But
in those long, frightening hours, when my down-
right mean grandmother confined me to "keep me out of her
way," I still had my Jesus. I'd sing the hymns I'd learned at
church, and when I didn't know the words, I'd make them up
and just keep going: "Jesus loves me, this I know, for the Bible
tells me so. Little ones to him belong; they are weak but he is
strong. . . ."

Today I speak to thousands of women who are locked in the
closet of their own pain. I know women struggle every day with
some hurt or another. I know because I've been there. In many

ways, I am *still there* because, frankly, life never lets up on this side of heaven. It's always something.

Like a mama longs to comfort her children, I want to gather all these wounded women in my audiences in my arms and rock them and sing lullabies of God's love to their wounded hearts — to embrace them with words of his comfort and hope.

But sometimes, girlfriends, real love has to be tough. And often, the most loving thing I can do is get in the face of somebody who is stuck on the floor of despair and tell them like it is.

And this is how it is: If you don't have the life you dreamed of, Honey, you better learn to love the life you've got.

It all starts with an attitude of gratitude.

Even when life is not what we hoped it would be, we can concentrate on the *good* things and what we *can* do. If we can walk and talk and see and smell and touch and taste — that's enough to keep us saying "thank you" to the Lord all day long.

I don't care if you're ill — you have something to be grateful for. You're still breathin', right? Thank God for the life you still have in the midst of your pain. While you're lyin' on your back, send praise songs and prayers to the ceiling and beyond — until your spirit breaks through to places where your physical body can't go anyway! (When praises go up, blessings come down.)

You've lost a loved one, you say, and now you can't find your way? Sweetheart, I say this in love: You are not the *first* and you will not be the *last* to walk through the valley of grief.

Can you move your arms and legs? Can you cry tears and wipe them away and love someone else who is hurting too? Thank the Lord for the grieving process, for the new awareness of life's fragility and how precious we are to one another. Tell someone you love them. Your job on earth ain't over till it's *over*.

Lost your job? Unless you live in a foreign country, you are not starving. In this country, if you can flip burgers, you can work. In America, when you're in trouble you can have a roof over your head and something to eat and find resources to help from any number of churches, good people, public libraries, and charitable organizations. Help is usually as close as a telephone call. Say a prayer of thanks and invite God to join in the adventure of meeting your family's needs.

Somebody has betrayed you, you say? Welcome to a part of the universal human experience. Sometime, somewhere, we will all feel betrayed. So what? Count the friends who *haven't* betrayed you, cling to the God who never leaves you, and be thankful for all that is right and beautiful in your life.

Think on those things that are good and beautiful and virtuous and true, and when you do, even though the problems are there, you have strength enough to deal with them and to get through them. Embrace life. Laugh! Brighten the world with the twinkle in your eyes and the smile on your lips. Speak aloud words of gratitude: for your family, for your God, for the brilliant colors in tonight's sunset, for a plate of hot, flaky, homemade biscuits. (I was once asked, "What's your favorite food,

Thelma?" And I quickly answered, "Anything that isn't tied down." So I could fill a praise notebook by simply listing the good foods I'm thankful to enjoy!)

When the world grows dreary and you are weary, come to him like a seven-year-old little girl. (Aren't we all really about seven years old on the inside anyway?) Then begin singing the simplest of affirming songs. "Jesus loves me, this I know ..."

Trust me on this, girlfriend. Ain't no closet so dark that his peace cannot invade it and light you up on the inside.

* *

This is the message we have heard from him and declare to you: God is light; in him there is no darkness at all.

1 JOHN 1:5

the friendship factor

Diana Pintar

. . . .

A sister is a friend and defender — a listener, a conspirator, a counselor, and a sharer of delights. And sorrows, too.

PAM BROWN

*W*ho's going to the hospital with you?" my friend Cindy asked.

"It's just a simple test," I said. "No big deal."

It *was* a big deal. The truth was, I was terrified. Something had gone horribly wrong with my swallow. I had forgotten how to do it. After several horrific choking episodes, I knew I had to act.

The scheduled test was a videofluoroscopy, a video X-ray that shows what is happening during a swallow. I was afraid I would either choke or have to expel unswallowed food (a polite word for "spit") during the test.

Under stress, I can be much like the Incredible Hulk. As Dr. Bruce Banner, Hulk's human counterpart, used to say, "I might get angry, and you won't like me when I'm angry." I did not want witnesses to *that*!

"I'll be fine, Cindy," I said, in what I hoped sounded like a "subject-closed" manner.

"I'm going!" she stated emphatically.

"Okay," I relented, realizing I needed a good friend to make it through this dreaded experience.

Cindy enthused, "We'll make a party out of it!"

A party! Only Cindy can turn a videofluoroscopy into a party. Every woman needs an encourager like Cindy.

Cindy began to plan our party with an essential concern. "What are you wearing?"

"A hospital gown, I suspect." I grinned.

"Oh, right!" Cindy paused and then blurted out, "Let's run over to Victoria's Secret and find some awesome underwear!"

"I don't think so, Cindy," I protested.

She countered, "We *have* to dress you up in some way!" She thought a moment. "How about a crown?"

I sat in stunned silence. Images ran through my mind of "glamorous me," parading through the hospital in the standard issue, backless hospital gown — with a crown upon my head. A smile was born deep in my heart. It wound its way up to my face, erasing every trace of fear. I laughed out loud.

"It sounds crazy!" I exclaimed. "But Cindy, *crazy* is exactly what I need right now!"

As the day approached, word of our "videofluoroscopy party" spread. Sandee, another friend who is a part of my circle of

Christian sisters, asked if she could join us. A third friend, Beth, decorated my crown with a Scripture verse, "I can do all things through Christ who strengthens me" (Philippians 4:13 NKJV).

When the big day arrived, as I sat waiting for my "chauffeurs" to arrive, my eyes fell on two helium balloons. They were remnants of my birthday, celebrated earlier that week.

"If I'm wearing a crown," I decided, gathering the balloons, "my friends are carrying these!"

Upon arrival, my friends presented me with a delightfully tacky Dollar Store crown, made of plastic, complete with big, garish fake rhinestones on the front. We paraded into the hospital, my entourage and I. I walked a bit ahead of them. Chin high, crown atop my head, I waved at startled onlookers, doing my best "Miss America" imitation. Cindy and Sandee walked a few steps behind, carrying the birthday balloons.

"What are you celebrating?" startled spectators inquired.

"Life!" we chortled.

I donned my gown and stored my clothes — all but my crown. When I emerged from the dressing room gowned, crowned, and ready to go, I was greeted by my giggling girlfriends — both of whom were attired in hospital gowns of their own.

Joy is contagious. Other patients joined our celebration. The waiting room resounded with laughter and happy noise.

When our "party pals" were called for their X-rays, they protested! Cindy, Sandee, and I bid them adieu like old friends.

"Good-bye! Good-bye! God bless!" we called after them as they left for their tests.

Then it was my turn.

"Diana Pintar?" the technician asked as she rounded the corner, chart in hand.

"That's me!"

She surveyed the scene. She read aloud the card that decorated my crown: "I can do all things through Christ who strengthens me." She smiled—a very big smile.

I am a woman of faith. I knew her smile was an indication that she was one of my Christian sisters too. I was greatly comforted.

The test began. I stood in the tiny X-ray room. Cindy, Sandee, and our new friend, the X-ray technician, stood in a small, glass-enclosed booth across the room.

"Let's start with the cracker on the right." The technician's instructions came through a speaker in the corner.

I felt alone. Fear returned. With shaking hands, I picked up the cracker. I tried. I failed. Hot tears flooded my eyes and began to wet my cheeks.

"This isn't working!" I protested.

"Diana," the technician called out, "remember what it says on your crown? 'I can do all things through Christ who strengthens me.'"

In the window, I could see Cindy, Sandee, and the X-ray technician. They were all smiling at me. Cindy and Sandee waved and clapped their hands. The X-ray technician gave me the thumbs-up sign.

Suddenly it did not matter if I passed or failed the test. This had been an amazing, joy-filled day! These women were more than friends; they were my sisters in Christ. Their support turned what could have been a devastating experience into one of my most delightful memories.

* *

It's better to have a partner than go it alone. Share the work,
share the wealth. And if one falls down, the other helps, . . .
By yourself you're unprotected. With a friend you can face
the worst. Can you round up a third? A three-stranded rope
isn't easily snapped.

ECCLESIASTES 4:9 – 12 MSG

when i had everything

Allison Shaw

Friendship improves happiness and abates misery by the doubling of our joy and the dividing of our grief.

CICERO

When I was a little girl, I hoped and wished and prayed for a sister, but I never got one. My mom told me that sometimes we have to adopt our sisters along the way. And so throughout my life, God has blessed me with some relationships that have transcended friendship to reveal a bond of sisterhood in Christ. Theresa belongs in that category.

I met Theresa after she and her husband, Jeremy, moved to Sacramento from South Carolina. As a California transplant myself, we shared the immediate bond of being far from home. When Theresa revealed that she was struggling in her marriage, I volunteered to meet with her weekly for prayer and accountability. I thought I was being a good friend. She needed me. But little did I know how much I would need her.

Within weeks of initiating our Monday evening accountability time, my husband, Michael, and I came under spiritual attack. We had some financial difficulty, Michael sprained his ankle, our car was stolen, and our apartment was robbed. Theresa was on her knees in prayer with me every step of the way. Often our friends see us at our best, for girls' nights or celebrations, but Theresa loved me when I was at my worst.

During my quiet time with the Lord one evening, I came across the stories in 1 Samuel that chronicle the friendship between David and Jonathan. It's a story that I was very familiar with, but it read differently this time around. It occurred to me that as King Saul's son, Jonathan *should* have been the next king of Israel. But even when David was anointed king and was promised everything that was rightfully Jonathan's, Jonathan still risked his life for David. It was such a vivid portrayal of friendship. I wondered if I could be that selfless for a friend.

When I told Theresa that I was expecting my first baby, she was ecstatic! For weeks we had prayed that we would be pregnant at the same time so that we could share the joys of motherhood together. What made her joy that much more precious was that Theresa had been trying to have a child for over a year with no success. I was amazed at her outpouring of love and excitement. As she jumped up and down, shrieking with glee for me, I realized that Theresa was just like Jonathan. Even when I was granted everything that she had ever desired, Theresa willingly laid aside her own sorrow to share in my happiness. She could have been angry, jealous, or resentful, but instead Theresa was selfless — a living example of Christ's love.

A few weeks later, Michael and I lost our precious baby, and it was Theresa who came to sit with me while I was overcome with grief. She brought flowers, bagels, cream cheese, and tea. She made me laugh when my heart was broken. But more important, she loved me with the love of a sister in Christ. All of those evenings on our knees before the throne of God, interceding for one another's burdens and praising the Father for our joys, had knit us together in a bond that transcended friendship.

Theresa says that before leaving South Carolina, she specifically prayed for a friend who would be an accountability partner, a prayer warrior, and a sister in Christ. Theresa's prayers were answered, and I am the one who was blessed.

Friends love through all kinds of weather, and families stick together in all kinds of trouble.

PROVERBS 17:17 MSG

gifts of the heart

Patricia Lorenz

. . . .

In every real adult, a child is hidden who wants to play.

FRIEDRICH NIETZCHE

When you're my age, more than half a century old, you don't get many bridal shower or wedding invitations from among your peers. Nieces and nephews, yes. Children of your friends, yes. But not too many wedding bells chime in my age category, especially among those who have already tied the knot once or twice before.

Therefore, when my friend Diane and her beloved Jack, who are even older than I am, decided to combine their love, lives, children, grandchildren, and the paraphernalia of three households (hers, her recently departed mother's, and his), the joy among friends and relatives resounded from state to state and across oceans.

In one fleeting dreamy-eyed moment during the planning of the wedding, Diane said wistfully, "Oh, I hope people don't bring presents. We do not need any more things. Our entire basement is filled, wall-to-wall, ceiling-to-floor, with things we don't need and can't possibly use in this lifetime. Nice things. Well, some of them are nice. Others are, well, too nice to throw away, but too sentimental to give to strangers. And I can't bear to have another rummage sale."

Diane kept talking and planning as she jabbered. "Wouldn't it be nice to give each guest who comes to our wedding a gift to take home instead of the other way around?"

I piped up, "Well, I'd be happy to give you a shower, and instead of playing those mindless games we could wrap all your treasures."

Diane practically shouted, "Yes! And then we'll give them away at the wedding! We'll number each present and I'll put corresponding numbers on each place card at the dinner tables at the reception."

And so the bridal shower invitations went out requesting that the women not bring gifts but rather gift wrap, tape, and scissors. At the house Diane and Jack had recently purchased, we gathered in the basement family room.

The first thing the shower attendees got to do was choose three or four gifts from the hundreds in the basement that we, personally, would like to own. We were commanded to take, take, take! It was more fun than 70-percent-off day at the nearest department store. As we chose the things we wanted for ourselves, Diane insisted that we take them to our cars immediately so they wouldn't get wrapped for the other wedding guests.

I chose a nice wooden tray that just needed a little lemon oil to remove the water stains, a small lead-crystal candy dish, and a china-faced floppy clown for my granddaughter.

Back downstairs after removing our own treasures, we giggling middle-aged women began to wrap the rest. There were candle holders wrapped in teddy bear paper. Picture frames and egg cups decorated in purple foil. Decanters in festive holiday paper. Jewelry and mugs in birthday florals. Housewares, glassware, trays, books, linens, silver, and bric-a-brac wrapped to the hilt. One hundred presents in all. "Enough to give a gift to everyone at the reception," Diane said, "with enough left over to share with the wait staff."

While we wrapped, ate, laughed, and talked about how we met Diane and what a joyous occasion this marriage would be, Jack sat upstairs wondering how his friends would perceive this crazy idea of handing out second-hand gifts at his wedding.

As I passed through the TV room where Jack was trying to ignore the cackling downstairs, I bubbled, "Jack, you're not going to believe how much stuff we're getting rid of! We're wrapping one hundred presents!"

"All I'm hoping for is an empty shelf downstairs where I can put a few of my own treasures," he mumbled.

"Jack, when we're finished, the entire basement will be cleaned out! You'll have tons of empty space!"

At the reception a few weeks later, Diane had written and printed a poem that was placed on every table. Two of the five stanzas declared,

> We love family and friends without measure.
> There are even some things that we treasure.
> But as three households merge, there are things we must
>   purge.
> So we gift them to you for your pleasure.
> You may keep them and use them — or not.
> You may love them or trash them or plot
> Ways to recycle them, give your own requiem.
> Love is wrapped in each piece in the lot!

And so it was that everyone who attended the revelry for the joining of two hearts left with a gift, a special remembrance of the lives of these two friends. And if I ever get married again, you can bet I'm going to follow in the tradition of my friend Diane and do the same thing. I think it ought to be the law, printed in bold letters in the Miss Manners handbook — especially if you're over forty and it's your second marriage.

....

It is more blessed to give than to receive.

ACTS 20:35

About Carol Kent, General Editor

Carol Kent is a popular international public speaker best known for being dynamic, humorous, encouraging, and biblical. She is a former radio show cohost and has been a guest on numerous television and radio programs. She is the president of Speak Up Speaker Services, a Christian speakers' bureau, and the founder and director of Speak Up With Confidence seminars, a ministry committed to helping Christians develop their communication skills. She has also founded the nonprofit organization Speak Up for Hope, which benefits the families of incarcerated individuals. A member of the National Speakers Association, Carol is often scheduled more than a year in advance for keynote addresses at conferences and retreats throughout the United States and abroad.

She holds a master's degree in communication arts and a bachelor's degree in speech education. Her books include: *When I Lay My Isaac Down, Becoming a Woman of Influence, Mothers Have Angel Wings, Secret Longings of the Heart, Tame Your Fears, Speak Up With Confidence*, and *Detours, Tow Trucks, and Angels in Disguise*. She has also cowritten with Karen Lee-Thorp *My Soul's Journey* and the *Designed for Influence Bible Studies*. Carol has been featured on the cover of *Today's Christian Woman* and her articles have been published in a wide variety of magazines. To schedule Carol to speak for your event, call 888-870-7719 or contact her at *www.SpeakUp SpeakerServices.com* or *www.CarolKent.org*.

About Thelma Wells

With upbeat, joyous enthusiasm Thelma Wells, popular author, international inspirational speaker, and businesswoman, offers heart-to-heart encouragement and assurances of God's personal intervention and direction in our lives. A speaker with Women of Faith, Thelma is president of A Woman of God Ministries and of Daughters of Zion Leadership Mentoring Program in Dallas. She is a professor at the Master's Divinity School in Evansville, Indiana. Her books include: *The Buzz, Bumblebees Fly Anyway*; *God Will Make A Way*; *What's Going On Lord?* and *Girl, Have I Got News for You!*

As an African-American woman, Thelma was instrumental in bringing racial diversity to the Women of Faith conferences. Through her ministry to thousands of women, Thelma believes she has found the fulfillment of a desire God has put in her heart and the culmination of a burning passion she has to share his love with women of all backgrounds.

Thelma is quick to point out there are more than 37,000 promises in the Bible. She is willing to share her own experiences of how Christ has kept his promises to her, and she is not afraid to call upon him in prayer to fulfill his promises. Whether it's her irrepressible spirit breaking through in her prayer life ("Am I supposed to keep asking you to do this, sir?") or a spellbinding vignette about a family member, Thelma's authentic passion for the Lord and faith in his love are ever present.

If it's encouragement and assurance you're looking for, Thelma's sharing it in abundance. And if you're hoping to discover God's promises, Thelma's delivering, for in our everyday circumstances, God will make a way! For additional information go to *www.thelmawells.com*.

Contributors

Charlotte Adelsperger is an author and speaker who has written for numerous publications, including *Focus on the Family, Clubhouse, Woman's World, Stories for the Heart,* and *Chicken Soup for the Soul.* Charlotte is a popular speaker at women's events and writers' conferences. Contact her 913-345-1678 or author04@aol.com.

Pauline Afman is the mother of Carol Kent, four more daughters, and a son. A master storyteller, she has been entertaining and encouraging her family and other audiences for much of her adult life. Pauline lives in Fremont, Michigan, and can be reached at: cpafman @ncats.net.

Sandi Banks' book *Anchors of Hope: Finding Peace Amidst the Storms of Life* offers hope to a hurting world. Her speaking will warm your heart, tickle your funny bone, and refresh your spirit. Sandi is director of Adult Worldview Conferences for Summit Ministries and served on the ACTS International board of directors. For information, contact Sandi at *www.anchorsofhope.com* or sandi@anchors ofhope.com.

Margaret K. Becker is an officer of Skyline Writers Club and the leader of the Christian Writer's Group of Greater Cleveland, Ohio. She has been published by *Decision* magazine and writes a "Gleanings" column for her church newspaper, *The Beacon.* She has three grown children, eight grandchildren, and six great-grandchildren.

Deborah P. Brunt writes a weekly column that appears in several newspapers, on numerous websites, and is distributed by email. She has written three books and contributed to several others. She is women's mssions and ministries specialist for Oklahoma Baptists. To receive Deborah's weekly columns by email, or for scheduling information, contact her at dbrunt@bgco.org or call 405-942-3800.

Karen Coy is the senior producer of the nationally syndicated television program *Aspiring Women*. She is also enjoying her new role as wife and stepmother to two teenaged boys. Karen serves on a worship team at her church and is a featured singer and speaker with the Spiritual Spa ministry events (*www.spiritualspa.org*).

Anne Denmark delights in using her spiritual gift of encouragement. Anne has a master's degree in adult education and a bachelor's degree in child development, with continuing education in floral design and clowning. She is a staff trainer with Speak Up With Confidence seminars, and her stories appear in *Mothers Have Angel Wings* and *Tame Your Fears*. Together with her husband, Don, she trains leaders of young married couples.

Jennie Afman Dimkoff is the president of Storyline Ministries Inc. and is the author of *Night Whispers: Bedtime Bible Stories for Women* and *More Night Whispers: Bedtime Bible Stories for Women*. She is also a speaker/trainer with Speak Up With Confidence seminars. For additional information, please visit her website at *www.JennieAfman Dimkoff.com*. To schedule Jennie as a speaker for your next event, call 888-870-7719.

Jeanne Doyon is a freelance writer, speaker, and encourager who desires to see women grow in Christ and recognize his fingerprints on their lives. She writes *The Stream's Edge*, a bi-monthly devotional newsletter, and hosts mini-retreats for high school girls.

Edna Ellison, known as "the Christian mentoring guru," is coauthor of *Woman to Woman: Preparing Yourself to Mentor* and *Seeking Wis-*

dom: Preparing Yourself to BE Mentored, both written with Tricia Scribner. Known for her humor and storytelling, Edna is a popular speaker. She has also written a series of Bible study books: *Friend to Friend*, *Friendships of Faith*, and *Friendships of Purpose*. For scheduling information, contact *www.womenbydesign.com*, or call 864-579-3328.

Bonnie Afman Emmorey is a speaker consultant with Speak Up Speaker Services and teaches communications skills for Speak Up With Confidence seminars and is helping launch Speak Up for Hope. For additional information, go to *www.SpeakUpSpeakerServices.com* and *www.SpeakUpForHope.com*.

Eva Marie Everson's work includes such titles as *Shadow of Dreams*, *Summon the Shadows*, and *Shadows of Light* as well as the 2005 releases *The Pot Luck Club* and *What Your Kids Won't Tell You*. Eva Marie speaks across the country at both writers' and women's conferences and retreats. She is a recent seminary graduate. For information, go to *www.EvaMarieEverson.com*. For scheduling information, call 888-870-7719.

Cathy Gallagher has been a salesperson, marketing manager, customer service director, assistant dean, and president of her own speaking and writing business. She has authored numerous articles for business and was the ghostwriter of a book on business communications. She is actively involved in a prayer ministry and a prison ministry through her church. Cathy speaks and writes on a wide variety of subjects. Contact Cathy to speak for your group by calling 888-870-7719.

Ginger Garrett is an author and speaker who has been encouraging women since 1995. Her books include *Moments for Couples Who Long for Children* and *Lose It for Life: Teens*, with Stephen Arterburn. You can visit her website and send her an email at *www.gingergarrett.com*.

Cheryl Gochnauer is the founder of Homebodies (*www.homebodies .org*), an online and print ministry for present and prospective stay-at-home moms, and author of *Stay-at-Home Handbook: Advice on Parenting, Finances, Career, Surviving Each Day & Much More*. To sign up for her free weekly email newsletter, email Cheryl@homebodies.org.

Judy Hampton is an international keynote speaker for women's conferences and the author of the book *Under the Circumstances*. For additional information, visit her website at *www.judyhampton.com*. To schedule Judy for your next event, call 888-870-7719.

Patricia Lorenz is an art-of-living writer and speaker and the author of five books, including her three latest, *Life's Too Short to Fold Your Underwear*, *Grab the Extinguisher*, *My Birthday Cake's on Fire*, and *Great American Outhouse Stories*. She's a top contributor to the *Chicken Soup for the Soul* books, the author of more than four hundred articles and stories, a contributing writer for fifteen Daily Guideposts books, and an award-winning newspaper columnist. Contact Patricia at patricialorenz@juno.com or at *www.PatriciaLorenz.com*.

Gracie Malone is a popular speaker and the author of *Off My Rocker — Grandparenting Ain't What It Used to Be* and *Still Making Waves — Creating a Splash in Midlife and Beyond*. Gracie's first book project, *Courage for the Chicken-Hearted*, coauthored with four friends, quickly became a best-seller. For speaking engagements, call 888-870-7719 or contact Gracie at *www.graciemalone.com* or at gracie@graciemalone.com.

Lucinda Secrest McDowell, a graduate of Gordon-Conwell Seminary, is an international conference speaker and author of *What We've Learned So Far*, *Amazed by Grace*, *Quilts from Heaven*, *A Southern-Style Christmas*, and *Women's Spiritual Passages*. She enjoys giving innovative presentations through her ministry, "Encouraging Words that Transform!" Contact her at *www.EncouragingWords.net* or at cindy@encouragingwords.net.

Shari Minke often portrays humorous characters, such as "Norma Lee Crotchety," a feisty, eighty-year-old preacher's wife; "Selma Kidds," a pregnant mom expecting her fourteenth child; and "Liza Little," a precocious five-year-old. Her biblical presentations and inspirational speaking will move you as much as her humor will delight you. Shari Minke can be contacted at 23870 Greening Dr., Novi, MI 48375, or at 248-348-5212.

Lynn D. Morrissey is author of *Love Letters to God: Deeper Intimacy through Written Prayer* and devotionals *Seasons of a Woman's Heart* and *Treasures of a Woman's Heart* and is a contributing author to numerous bestsellers. She is on staff with CLASS and is an Advanced Writers and Speakers Association speaker, specializing in prayer journaling and women's topics. Contact Lynn at words@brick.net.

Diana Pintar is the president of the Next Step Ministries Inc. and travels nationally as a speaker for women's conferences and retreats. Diana is a speaker/trainer with Speak Up With Confidence seminars. For additional information, visit her website at *www.TheNextStepOnline.com*. To schedule Diana as a speaker for your next event, call 888-870-7719.

Danika Protzman has been an educator in both international and domestic schools for the past twelve years. She is currently home schooling her three children. She seeks to inspire others in personal spiritual growth through speaking engagements, devotions, and prayer. For additional information, visit her website at *www.deeper heartministries.org*.

Cynthia Reynolds served as a missionary in Europe with her husband and three children. She edited a newsletter for missionary women and currently writes "Bequest of Wings," a literary review newsletter. She speaks to missionary families and encourages creativity as a form of worship. She enjoys reading, writing, and all things creative. Cynthia lives in Madison, Wisconsin, and can be contacted at cynkreynolds@charter.net.

Laurie Winslow Sargent is the author of *The Power of Parent-Child Play* and *Delight in Your Child's Design*. She has written for dozens of magazines, including *Parenting*, *Today's Christian Woman*, and *Writer's Digest*; is PR chairman for the *Northwest Christian Writers Association*, and speaks frequently to parent and writers' groups. Contact Laurie at *www.ParentChildPlay.com*.

Allison L. Shaw is a freelance writer and editor from Sacramento, California. She is passionate about children's literature, her career as a librarian, and her husband, Michael. Her published work appears in the *Sacramento Bee*, several anthologies, and pages scattered throughout the World Wide Web. To contact Allison, write to allie_shaw@hotmail.com or call 916-366-3021.

Ginger Shaw is a communications trainer for Speak Up With Confidence seminars. She is a playwright and an actress who has frequently appeared on *Turning Point* with Dr. David Jeremiah. For information on scheduling Ginger to speak at your next leadership training seminar or women's conference, call 888-870-7719.

Debi Stack is a speaker to women's groups and radio audiences on the topics of stress, perfectionism, and over-commitment, and author of *Martha to the Max: Balanced Living for Perfectionists*. For additional information, visit her website at *www.maxedout.net*. To schedule Debi as a speaker for your event, call 800-433-6633.

Rachel St. John-Gilbert is author of *Wake Up Laughing: Offbeat Devotions for the Unconventional Woman*. She's wife to Scott and mother to Trevor, Tori, and Whitney. She loves to answer reader email between settling skirmishes over toys and making PB&J sandwiches. She can be reached at *www.rachelstjohngilbert.com*.

Melissa S. Sutter lives in Grant, Michigan, with her husband and her two sons. A graduate of Central Michigan University, Melissa taught high school for eleven years. She is the principal at Grant Christian School and is Coffee Break director at a nearby church. She also co-leads the Caring Ministry team and leads the Women's Ministry team at Bailey Christian Church. Melissa writes short stories, skits, and organizational tips for Coffee Break. She has been published in *Encounters with God*.

Vicki Tiede is a wife, mother, teacher, and motivational speaker. For additional information, visit her website at *www.GraceLessons .com*. To schedule Vicki as a speaker, contact her at Vicki@Grace Lessons.com or by phone at 507-254-5656.

Penny Williams is a psychologist and conference speaker. She is the president of Center for Positive Living counseling centers in Lansing and Jackson, Michigan. The emphasis of her practice is on biblically based Christian counseling for children, couples, families, and individuals. Visit her website at *www.center4positiveliving.org*.

Jeanne Zornes is a women's retreat and conference speaker and a writer of hundreds of articles and seven books, including *When I Prayed for Patience ... God Let Me Have It!* She lives in Washington State. Contact her at P.O. Box 4362, Wenatchee, WA 98807-4392.

kisses of sunshine

Hardcover
0-310-24766-7

Hardcover
0-310-24846-9

Hardcover
0-310-24765-9

Hardcover
0-310-24767-5

Hardcover
0-310-24768-3

Pick up a copy today at your favorite bookstore!

ZONDERVAN™

GRAND RAPIDS, MICHIGAN 49530 USA

WWW.ZONDERVAN.COM

We want to hear from you. Please send your comments about this book to us in care of zreview@zondervan.com. Thank you.

ZONDERVAN™

GRAND RAPIDS, MICHIGAN 49530 USA

WWW.ZONDERVAN.COM